Becoming the Successful Mortgage Broker

DISCLOSURE

Becoming the Successful Mortgage Broker

JASON C. MYERS

WWW.PALMETTOPUBLISHINGGROUP.COM

Palmetto Publishing Group, LLC
Charleston, SC

For more information regarding special discounts for bulk purchases, please contact Palmetto Publishing Group at Info@PalmettoPublishingGroup.com.

ISBN-13: 978-1-944313-09-8
ISBN-10: 1-944313-09-5

Table of Contents

Prologue

This is now the second book in our series, and based upon initial feedback, we are seeing that the biggest questions about our industry come from two sources. The first group of questions comes from newer mortgage brokers, and these are questions regarding how to build their businesses. The second group of questions comes from bankers who are looking to become brokers, and how to make that transition successfully.

With this second book, I will break up the information in to three different parts. Part one of this book will be geared more toward newer mortgage originators and brokers, and will contain information on how to do things, and how to get started in the mortgage brokerage industry. Part two of this book will cover various sales techniques that will be useful to any loan officer or mortgage broker. Part three, the final section of the book, I've set aside to cover information for bankers who are wanting to transition in to being mortgage brokers. This section will also contain information about opening your own "one-man," or smaller-sized, mortgage shop.

The sales techniques provided here have been compiled based on communication I've received from all types of bankers and brokers in our industry. In addition, some techniques can also be found on my website (www.jasoncmyers.com) via our site's newsletters and archives. If you have any questions or communication for me, please feel free to contact me via e-mail: info@jasoncmyers.com.

Thank you in advance for the support and interest in my work, and I look forward to continued communication and helping my fellow brokers around the country. Let's all stay positive, and keep building a network of professionals that represents the quality inherent to our industry.

SECTION 1:

Getting Started

1

Licensing

THE MOST SWEEPING changes that happened regarding licensing in our industry came about via Dodd Frank and the creation of the NMLS, or National Mortgage Licensing System. This created both a standard and a registry for loan officers that had never previously existed. Getting started in the industry now is really rather simple. The following website—mortgage.nationwidelicensing-system.org—will help you get started.

On the home page, you will see there are two options: one is to get started as a company, and the other is to get started as a mortgage originator. Both options are located inside blue boxes, front and center. For our purposes, we will focus on the mortgage originator link, and this will take you a screen that will allow you to create a unique username and password for yourself. Once you have set up your username and password, you have created your future landing page for your testing, licensing, and continuing education. Most of the information found on the home page gives you updates for various states.

The first step will be to focus on your current home state, assuming that is the place where you want to do business. This will let you know what various steps you'll need to take to become licensed in your home state. All states require the national licensing test, or SAFE test, and all states will have, at the very least, a national level background check as a requirement. Be aware that some states will require individual, state-level background checks, along with ongoing continued education. Generally, your first year will consist of taking the SAFE test, along with most state's required minimum of roughly eight hours of specific continuing education. Some states like Colorado and North Carolina also require two hours of unique, state-level continuing education.

Across the top of the home page you will see links for items such as news and events, professional standards, state licensing, reports, resources, and resources/support. All of these links are very good sources of information for a new loan officer. The log-in for loan officer is in the top right corner of the home page. There are also some quick links in the bottom right corner, which include the NMLS consumer access, federal guidelines, and training workshops. There is also a newsletter link in the bottom, left-hand corner, and I would recommend that a new loan officer sign up for it in order to keep you connected to licensing changes. This newsfeed information will keep you in the loop as far as what's going on in the world of licensing. There are also places to link to an upload your continuing education (CE) certificates, and banner ads that will keep you informed about workshops, seminars, etc. At the top of the home page there are links to contact NMLS, as well as a quick-search box that can help answer questions. While that may not sound exciting, it is very important to know about anything that could affect your ability to close a loan.

The most important thing to remember about your licensing is that it is ultimately up to the individual loan officer to remain in compliance with their specific license requirements. Your company will also be responsible for maintaining its state company licensing. You have to have both pieces in place to originate a loan in any state. It is very much a two-part system. You have to be both sponsored by a financial institution with a valid company and branch license, as well as your individual license.

So, for example, if John Smith has licenses in Virginia, Colorado, and Maryland, and he goes to work for Good Experience Home Loan, he has to make sure each state license is something offered by his sponsoring company. Good Experience Home Loan will have to apply for and maintain state licenses in all three states, as well as pay the fees to have a branch license in each state. The main purpose of branch licensing per each state is frankly so the state knows where to find the loan officer in case they need communicate or send mail, and when there's the case of an audit, be able to send auditors.

Let's talk about the consequences of licensing issues. All states have finally gotten on board with having annual renewals done on the same date at the end of the year: December 31. If you do not complete renewals, continuing education , or pay fees, or if your company does not, then your license will automatically terminate on this date. It makes it very important that you maintain the necessary CEs, and that you renew your licenses within the required time limits.

If you choose to no longer do business in a particular state, it is very important that you close out the license properly. This means notifying the state, and either changing the license to inactive or terminated, status. Failure to do so will lead to potential fines for you or your company. At the moment we're going to focus on the individual loan officer, but we'll address company licensing further on in the book. For now, the most important thing to keep in mind is that *your license is your responsibility.*

Also keep in mind that with the new expiration date of December 31, most states have a renewal policy that allows you to renew any states you may have missed up to January 31. If you miss a state renewal, you have a period where you can still renew, but you will typically pay an additional late fee. If you go past January 31, then you are looking at a completely new application, accompanied by all new background checks and fees.

The typical turnaround time for getting a state license varies state to state. I have seen it take as short as one month, but as long as four months. It is easier to maintain and pay for the licenses once you have them, than it is to start fresh on new states each year. The key for mortgage originators is to have this make sense for you financially. The cost for loan officers is typically minimal, while the cost per state in terms of bonding and licensing is much more expensive for a company.

All of your licensing is also contingent on the bonding of the company you work for, and, depending on where you are licensed as a broker or correspondent, there a different type of bond. The bonding for a correspondent is more expensive. A few states, most notably Colorado, require the individual loan officer to have a bond.

Keep in mind that in order for a licensed loan officer to do business in a state, they have to be both active with their licensing *and* sponsored by a valid company. You can run in to issues if the company license expires, surety bonds don't renew, or any number of items occur at this time period. Make sure you know what the company plans are for that state prior to renewal periods. The NMLS system is still improving in a number of areas, and it really is a benefit to the overall health of our industry. The biggest improvement is the creation of the NMLS consumer access portal, which can be found here: mlsconsumeraccess.org.

The creation of this website is an accountability factor for loan officers. This website allows all the individuals with access to the Internet to look up any loan officer and check the loan officer's status. It provides information such as which states the loan officer is licensed in, and when his or her license was obtained. It also shows whether you are eligible to work in a specific state, or if your company is not active. This system is also used by investors to check and make sure all licenses are in place prior to allowing a loan officer to close, or originate, a loan. This will come up in January each year if you have loans in process, or if there are any delays in renewal. The consumer access portal is also a reporting system for any regulatory action. This brings us to a conversation about consent orders.

Consent orders can be severe, and they can also come about for something simple, like failing to file a proper request to change the status of a license to inactive. Consent orders are the way for a state to end a relationship with a loan officer or his company. This is important because if this happens to a company, nobody who works for that company can originate in that particular state going forward. I have experience both types of consent orders, and I recommend that if, at any point, you are dealing with the state, make sure you have legal representation, and make sure you have done all that is within your power to comply with the state's requests. The good news is that a consent order in one state isn't necessarily a death sentence in another state. The states do not typically follow each other in this respect. I do strongly suggest that you avoid consent orders at all cost, but if you find yourself in this situation you need to hire an attorney who specifically understands these rules, and you need to do your best to pay any fines so the matter is resolved.

The licensing for any loan officer is ultimately the loan officer's lifeblood, and their careers hinge up it, so there is a need for them to watch all industry changes, and to keep their licenses active and in place. Without a license you cannot originate loans, or commissions associated with those loans. Take good care of your license, and it will take good care of you.

2

Education

FOR A NEW loan officer, there can never be enough education, and any number of sources can help with getting started. First let's try to organize what information we need, and where to source it, when starting out.

First and foremost, you will have had to train and study enough to pass the national SAFE test. You can order study materials and receive online support from many sources, like this one: www.trainingpro.com. We, personally, have someone who comes in to train anyone who is becoming a loan officer. I feel that the material is so in-depth now, that having a guide for the questions is the best route. Once you pass the SAFE test through a local testing agency, you will then need to pass your individual state testing. I recommend you do not start your state testing until after you pass the SAFE course. The reason for this is pretty simple:

You don't want to confuse state specific information with the national level testing. In my experience, the state test involves far more dates and regional information that varies from state to state. If you are going to take advantage of the multi-state licensing, you will want to get individual state study guides, which can also be found online through multiple sources.

The key with individual states is that you need to come up with a game plan, and coordinate that with the availability of the states from the firm you work for as a loan officer. If you look on the NMLS website you can get an idea of the costs associated with each state, and then use that as a road map to the states you may want to apply for as a mortgage professional. Costs, along with the type of marketing you will be doing, should be factored in to your decision to get additional licenses. If you have a marketing plan that involves focusing only on purchase business, then you may just need the license in your home state. If you have a game plan that involves taking your marketing to a national or regional level, then you will need additional licensing. As a component of the SAFE test, you also get access to almost all states, but you will have to have the education level necessary if they need additional CE, and then apply for those states in which you want to be licensed.

Once you are licensing in your home state, remember that this is a process that can take, on average, about a month. The single largest delay is usually the background check. I would suggest that anyone who wants to fast track their licensing get the background check out of the way as soon as possible. Typically we require someone to pass the SAFE test before we go to the expense of getting a background check. The background check does require you to go to a local police station or fingerprinting center to get your finger prints done, and to then submit them to the state. Also pay attention when it comes to some states, like Georgia, that require both a national-level background check (FBI check) and a state-specific background check. Again, all of this information is available on NMLS.

Now that you have achieved your licensing, and you are ready to begin work as a mortgage broker, keep in mind that only part of your education has taken place. The next steps, and the next levels of education, involve learning your operating system as well as specific investor product knowledge. Let's next discuss the common operating systems found in mortgage origination.

The two most common operating systems are Calyx Point and Encompass. These two systems are similar, but both have features to consider. First and foremost, you probably won't have much say-so when it comes to which system is used. The operating system will be a decision made by your employer, or, if you are starting out on your own, you will then get to choose and will most likely select a system you're familiar with from the past. These two systems are the most widely used systems in the mortgage broker side of the equation.

There are a lot of similarities when you look at the two different systems. Encompass has more marketing and client relationship management tools, and they are all user friendly. In my opinion, however, Calyx Point is the more user-friendly system, and it is the system I have used from day one in the industry. It is pretty much all about mortgages—and I mean that in a good way. It is a daily operating system that does not try to be something other than what it is, such as a CRM or task manager. The downside is that you need to use a different system or link management software to *point* at an additional cost, but I have found that doing so is the better strategy due to the range of material and products available from outside venders.

Calyx is there to organize and process your application. It also has plenty of features to keep you in compliance, and to run your loan scenarios through LP (Freddie Mac) and DU (Fannie Mae). This is plenty enough operating system for someone getting started, and it is easy to learn. Calyx offers webinars and online training, as well as customer support. These same features can be found in Encompass as well. Some of the lesser known, but nevertheless still used, operating systems include ones like the Byte Operating System. I am not as familiar with these systems, but that does not mean they are not also effective.

The key to any of these systems is to take advantage of the education they offer so that you can speed up your learning curve to allow you to complete the full application. Always go back to the single most important task of any loan officer, which is to complete the *full application.*

One key decision you will need to make is whether to become a banker or a broker. The key difference between these two is that a banker is typically set up as a correspondent lender. This means that, if you are a banker, you will lend in your own name, and you will have defined products. A broker will lend in the name of their investor, and will typically have more niche products to offer. You can be both, depending on the type of license you acquire. In the state of South Carolina, we have two unique license types, and two different standards for loan officers depending on their type of employment. Other states have similar distinctions and different rules, so it is important to make sure you have the right type of licensing for the type of lender you plan on being going forward.

What are the advantages and disadvantages of each? Well, both models follow some type of comp plan for individual loan officers, so in this respect they are similar to one another. If you are the owner of your own company, there are advantages to a banker-based model due to the higher compensation that is available. I will go in to more detail regarding this in the section that addresses owning your own shop. For individual loan officers, the key advantage when it comes to the banker model, is that you will become familiar with your underwriters, as this is a common feature for correspondent lenders. A full correspondent lender will, typically in-house, underwrite all products they will be funding on their warehouse line. A mini-correspondent will typically use the same investors who will underwrite. A broker will not be an underwriter, and will instead have the investor do the underwriting, and will close in their name.

There are pluses and minuses to both aspects of this type of lending. If you have one set of underwriting guidelines, you may not be able to do every loan. An example of this would be if your company only goes down to 640 or 620 credit scores, which would eliminate all loans for borrowers with credit scores below this threshold. Other lenders may have lower standard scores. A downside for brokers is that they typically do not control the issuing of documents or funds, so they can see potential delays depending on the investor. A big plus for a broker is that they will be able to offer niche products, and receive a guaranteed compensation. All of these type of loan officers have strengths that make them viable options for when you are just getting started in the business. The important thing is for you to pick which option is the best fit for you in your particular market. Important factors to consider are the support they give you as a loan officer, the team you are joining, and, if you are on your own, the level of support from the investors.

Once you are serviceable enough with your operating system, then comes the final, most important aspect of your education. Product knowledge establishes the difference between an order taker and a loan officer. You will see the difference in the level of volume you are able to close when you are able to offer numerous options to your clients. While some companies like Guaranteed Rate and Quicken are trying very hard to automate the mortgage industry with online decisions and Rocket Mortgages, it will be the mortgage professional on the ground who can clearly walk clients through the individual loan scenario who will end up with the business in the long run. Every loan scenario is different, and you need to know your products in order to know what you can and cannot offer to your clients. The best source of product knowledge will be your account representatives for your investors. While getting started, you need to meet as many AE's as possible and see which ones your company offers. Keep in mind that if you are going to a correspondent lender, your options may be limited, or hidden behind pricing software. In this case, you will need to know exactly what types of loans you can offer based upon credit rating, debt to income levels, and any niche products. Most likely if you have gone correspondent, you will have a selected comp plan, and this may or may not limit some of your brokerage options. What I've observed, is that anything that is fairly standard will fall into a standard comp plan for you as a loan officer. Anything that has to be brokered will most likely result in a lower comp plan. The reason for this is simple: The correspondent lender typically sells all their own loans, giving them a pricing advantage. If they have to broker the loan, this means they too have a comp plan in place with that investor, and it limits the profitability of that loan to the company. For individuals that are acting truly as brokers, there will be more options and more investors, all with different ranges of set comp plans. The account representatives are there to help you close loans, and a good AE can be worth his or her weight in gold. One key aspect you want to pick up on, is which AEs are able to get stuff done for you, and which ones are run by their back office. One trend I've seen is less in-person representation by the investors, and more going to the call center variety of support. So you will have one dedicated AE, but you may never meet him or her in person, as they are based out of a home office somewhere else. This can be a good and a bad thing, because they may be harder to reach, and you may not get the personal interaction you desire. A good AE does not have to show up once a week to your office, but it can be helpful to put a face with a name and voice. If you are getting started out, this can also help you build a familiarity with the investor and their products. When dealing with an AE, don't be afraid to ask questions, because that is honestly what they are there for, and it is their job. Also, don't be afraid to sign up for newsletters and e-mail blasts. You can always unsubscribe later if you don't find any valuable content. Being connected does help you stay in touch with product offerings, and keep you abreast of any news about what is going on within the industry. This will all contribute to your level of education.

Finally, as far as ongoing education, you'll need to take continuing education each and every year. Don't be afraid to sign up for more CE than you need, because there are valuable pieces out there. You also want to sign up for at least one daily or weekly newsletter. Some examples of these are Rob Chrisman's or Mortgage News—both of which will keep you in the loop. If you are starting out as a broker with your own shop, you must sign up for the Scotsman Guide, which will keep you in the loop about new products, industry trends, and key investor contact information. You can register for Rob Chrisman's daily newsletter by going to his website (www.robchrisman. com), and the other example, Mortgage News Daily, can be found here: www.mortgagenewsdaily.com.

Kaizen is a Japanese word that means "to improve daily in all aspects." One of my first employers used this concept, and still uses it as his motto to this day. It really is a good idea, and is exactly the way a loan officer should look at the industry. We can all learn something new each day; the key is knowing how to access the information available that will help us to become the best mortgage professionals.

3

Tips for a New Loan Officer

STARTING OUT IN our industry right now is not that easy. We have touched on licensing and education requirements already, and the bar has been raised considerably. I would strongly suggest that someone planning to enter our industry have a strong financial, marketing, or business background in college or technical school. I have found that the software we use makes it easier to understand the actual math of the process, but one can prepare for the marketing and technical aspects via higher education.

This section is designed for someone who is starting out in our industry, but it never hurts for even someone with more seniority to look back over some basics. Kind of like fielding ground balls—it never hurts to have practice. You also need to think of yourself as a sponge, and soak up as much information and knowledge as you can at every turn.

Training is pretty much going to be done on the job, and—for lack of a better phrase—you have to "break some eggs to learn how to make an omelet." I suggest all new loan officers, once properly licensed, focus on refinances as the first line of lending you do for training purposes. I have had far more success starting loan officers on refinances versus starting them off on purchase business. The simple reason for this is that purchases have deadlines, realtors, sellers, and numerous other potential pitfalls. A newer loan officer is not prepared to handle the coordination of all the various factors in a purchase. I usually train my loan officers for a minimum of a year on mailer, Internet leads, and past clients. Not everyone will have a past client list as extensive as we have, but you can create a mailer system and purchase Internet leads. Starting out, a loan officer will need some assistance in one of these areas in order to become successful. I do not recommend any new loan officers to try to flag down a ton of purchase business. Reputation is all you have in the industry, and as soon as you have one or two bad closings with a realtor, you can pretty much consider that a lost relationship unless you have other ties to that realtor (such as family, friends, or lead system).

Education in general can be done online through various sites, including places such as www.trainingpro.com

or www.mortgageeducation.com. This type of education and training will only get you so far, given the amount of changing conditions across the industry. Really, the absolute best way for someone to get started is to work as a junior support person, or as an assistant to a high-volume loan officer. The reality is that banks are not really looking to hire a ton of people who are fresh to the industry, and are instead moving to automate as much of the lending process as possible to allow fewer people to handle more volume. I think if you asked most banks, they would assume they have nothing but underwriters and processors in order to keep costs down, but the reality is that a good mortgage broker is a professional who can navigate tricky underwriting rules, have superior product knowledge, and offer better rates (lower costs) to the consumer. There is no substitute for working on deals in our industry, and the compliance piece of the equation almost makes a role as an apprentice or an assistant an absolute must when first getting down in to the trenches. That being said, there are some simple ways you can build your brand, so let's look at some of the things you can do to get started, whether you are working under a senior loan officer, or if you are starting out on your own. Keep in mind that, from a licensing standpoint, in order to own your own shop, you have to meet the required minimum number of years in terms of industry experience prior to opening your own shop. These techniques are simple and cost effective ways to jump start your business.

Building a list is not as hard as it seems. Basically everyone is online now, and you can build a list with a little time and an excel spreadsheet. The key is to find the right group for the type of marketing you want to do, and to then build and maintain this list over time. Whether you do hard-copy mailing or e-mail, you will need to keep your list up to date, and to make sure you are not missing your mark. Whenever you build a list, make it as complete as possible. Since we are most likely talking about building a list for realtors at some point, you will want to include their phone numbers on the list, and then give them a call to follow up after any mail you may have sent. Again, the good news here is that most realtors will be online, and you can access good contact information for them.

Appearance in business is your first impression on any client or business associate. I was once told to get a Brooks Brothers catalog, and make myself look like the people in the catalog if I wanted to do business as a financial advisor. I find that to still be true, and that is the easiest example I can use to help with someone who is just getting started. Get a Brooks Brothers catalog, and shop there. As a new loan officer, you need to look professional, be well kept and groomed, with a pressed shirt, tie, and shiny shoes. You do not yet have the knowledge to wow everyone in a telephone setting, so you need to present yourself as a business professional.

One secret I will let you in on, is, if you are using mailers or telephone sales for the most part to start, guess what? You will not actually be meeting face to face with most clients. This presents a second front for you to present yourself. With telephone sales, the key is for you to speak clearly and, more importantly, *slowly*. This is your opportunity to sell something, but keep in mind that with both Internet and mailer leads, they are calling in to you, or you are fulfilling a request. You do not need to over sell anything, and you should instead take the approach of listening. Ask a lot of questions. One very key basic to telephone sales is to get the client talking and to then let them keep talking. You want to take them through a natural progression. With telephone sales for a mortgage, you want to keep it simple, and quickly determine if the client is going to be of such quality as to warrant spending your time on. To this end, I have broken down an incoming call for a mailer. There will be a slight variation when it comes to Internet leads, which I will go over secondly. Keep in mind, you should know in advance the type of mailer call or Internet lead, and the reason they'll calling you. For this example we will use the scenario of an FHA client calling to potentially remove mortgage insurance.

1. There is an incoming call. The first step is to answer your phone, and to introduce yourself and your company.

2. "Are you calling on one of our mailers?" Most clients will say they are calling on something they received in the mail. Your answer should always be, "That's great news for you!" Be very positive.

3. Next comes the most important step. You need to cut to the chase. Too often I hear loan officers start rambling at this point in the call. In telephone sales, especially on a mailer or Internet lead, you need to get to the point. Tell your client, point blank, that you have two questions, and their answer can tell you if whether to continue is worth your time. Selling a refinance deal, you need to have about a point in reduction, or, in this case, the value to remove the mortgage insurance. So with an FHA conversion, you would have one follow-up question: "What is your loan amount and your interest rate?" The question, "What is your address?" is the second question, but with a mailer type only.

4. What this does is immediately tell you whether or not the client has the opportunity to be worth the time to do a refinance. Don't be scared to tell someone there is no value in continuing your call. There is no point in wasting both their time and yours, and you really don't want to fatigue yourself with a sales pitch to a client of no value. It does not do you, or

the client, any good to talk for thirty minutes if you can't save someone money on a refinance. That is the whole reason they are calling you to begin with: They are interested in either checking current market conditions, or saving a few bucks.

5. The next step is, once you have the address, you need to be by your computer to quickly check the value either by using a prepaid system or a free site like Zillow. I used Zillow, and it is actually a feature tied in to lead mailbox. Keep in mind, I have found Zillow values to be off by 10 percent too low in urban areas and by 10 percent too high in rural areas. Factor this into your number, and quickly do some math. If the loan amount is below 80 percent of the estimated value, then you now have a prospect worth talking to on the line.

6. Quickly move into a positive sales approach, and tell your potential client the good news, or in a scenario where you have no value there, you can check to see if an alternative program, such as an FHA streamline, would be of value. Alternatively, you can also politely end your call.

7. If you have a quality prospect on the phone line, then you immediately ask them if they would like

to go into the application process. You may be met with some resistance, but keep in mind, they called you to find out information. If they are ready, you stay on the phone with them as long as possible to build a rapport, all the while taking your mortgage application in the process. If they are not able to do the application at that point, immediately set a time when you'll call them back, and then set a reminder for yourself to call them later.

8. Once you have your application to start your mortgage process, you will always want to follow up with an e-mail thanking your new client that provides them with your complete contact information, including your cell phone number. Starting out, you will always need to be accessible to your clients. As you grow, and as your business grows, you will be able to use assistants to help you follow up and contact clients, but when you are coming out of the gate, you need to be the lead at all times.

9. Also, something very simple but often overlooked, is thanking your client for the opportunity to earn their business. This is a person that is trusting you to do work for them, so thank them for the chance.

Internet leads will have a little different feel to them if you are calling a lead from Lower My Bills or a lead from Lending Tree. The main difference, and obstacle, will be getting the client on the phone. I tell my loan officers who are working Internet leads that there are only three acceptable answers with a lead: "Yes, I am going with you"; "No, I am going with someone else"; or "Quit calling." You can never call an Internet lead too many times. The reason I say this is very basic: the cost associated with that lead. On average, a good response ratio for conversion to deals is going to be 4 percent, or 4 out of a hundred. I tend to see closer to 8 percent, or 8 out of a hundred. You might ask why, but it's because I keep calling—over and over and over again—until I get one of the three answers I just listed. I also use a sales scorecard, which you'll find following this chapter, and you will see that it really is a numbers game at all times. I used the scorecards with all my younger loan officers, because the numbers don't lie. If you put in the work and make the calls, you will see results.

Let's look at the specifics of an Internet-based call. The Internet lead can be as filtered, or as complete as possible, depending on cost. I will only purchase exclusive leads. That's not to say that the client hasn't gone out somewhere else, but I will only purchase and call an Internet lead that is given to us, and only us. The reason is simple: There is already a lot of competition in our market place, so why pay for something that you know is being sold to two or three other people at the same time? Exclusive leads may cost more, but they are worth it. I also look for highly filtered leads that come with as much information as possible. Again, these may cost more, but I can tell you that if you follow the first steps and call relentlessly, it will pay off with more loans in your pipeline. I have found the truth to be that you get what you pay for with Internet leads. A three-dollar lead is typically only going to be worth just that—three dollars. You should purchase the highest quality lead you can afford, and always look to be able to commit to a hundred leads at a time. This makes them easy to track, and easy to see how you are doing. On average, I pay about fifty bucks per lead, so for five thousand dollars, I expect to see roughly eight deals, which make, on average, three to five thousand dollars. That is a very good return for Internet leads. When signing up for an Internet lead service, be aware of any minimums, and make sure you have a delivery method that comes directly to your phone or computer. Also make sure you have the ability to not receive leads if you are not able to work them. The key factor with any Internet lead is response time. You need to call the lead within minutes of having received it. If you wait, chances are, they've filled out multiple online searches, and your money will be wasted when they go with a competitor because you didn't call them.

In terms of what you say to your lead once you get them on the phone, again, we want to go with a simple method. The sales technique for this type of call needs to be more like taking someone's order. I use more a presumptive close if we have a rate that works. This is the way I filter my leads: I typically always know the rate they have listed, or some basic facts, such as whether they are doing cash out, etc. Always prep prior to making the call. It only takes a few seconds, and it can make or break your sale.

10. Introduce yourself, your company, and, most importantly, the lead source. If you are calling from a lead from XYZ Cash out.com, then you need to identify that so they know what the call is in reference to, and why you are calling them. Quickly say, "For security purposes, I need to confirm you…"

11. Get a few easy pieces of information from them, such as confirming their address, loan amount, full name, and interest rate. These are questions you already know the answer to, but you want to get the client to start saying yes to some easy questions. Also, you want to identify that the person with whom you are speaking actually put the request out there. If you are speaking to a spouse, or someone that did not make the request, you need to quickly request information that will get you in touch with that person. There is no reason to pitch to someone who isn't the one making the decision.

12. After doing the quick confirmation, you will want to have your rate prepared with their potential savings. You also want to ask them what exactly it is they want to accomplish with a refinance. This very simple question could lead you down a path to where you're able to get them a solution. I say this because in some cases the rate they listed in the lead may be of no real benefit, and your initial thought process will be to dismiss this lead as worthless. That may or may not be the case, so you need to ask the question. The answers will surprise you. I have seen everything from them needing cash out to pay for college to hating their current lender and wanting to refinance away from them. There could be any number of things going on, from divorce, getting out of a reverse mortgage after a primary borrower pasted away, to just plain debt consolidation. All of these answers would be missed if you don't take the time to ask the question. As the saying goes, don't judge a book by its cover.

13. Once you determine whether or not you have something of value, and the quality of the client, move into the application, and take your time. Fill in all the blocks in the application. If the answer is zero, then put in a zero. Do not leave anything blank on the mortgage application.

The single most important thing a new loan officer should learn to do correctly is complete the *full application.* I would say 75 percent of processing delays are caused by incomplete applications. What is the definition of complete? Well, that is simple. Every single box in your standard 1003, or online software, should be filled in with something, whether that be a number or a zero or a yes or a no. How to ensure the application is complete is simple: keep the client on the phone and ask all the questions on the mortgage application. Take the time, and do it right the first time. A new loan officer has to think of the loan application as a road map. If you give bad directions, you will have bad results, and people will get lost along the way. These are some of the key areas that I often see loan officers haven't completed, which causes a delay:

- Incomplete Income: If your borrower has a paystub with several forms of income, including expenses, sick days, or overtime, you need to break the income down, and in most cases get a written verification of employment
- Incomplete "Real Estate Owned" Section: You need to fill out all pieces of information for any other property owned by your borrowers, including the taxes, insurance, and HOA fees for the subject and rental property

- Understated or Missing Assets: This can go both ways. If you have a deal that is close, you will want to get as many assets as possible. If you have the bulk of your assets in one or two accounts, you can minimize the documentation for your client by focusing in on just those accounts. I tell all my loan officers to take all the information into account during your initial application, and you can always take it back out later.
- Missing Retirement Assets
- Incorrect Disclosure of Past Credit Issues, like Foreclosure or Bankruptcy
- Missed Alimony or Child Support Payments
- Incorrect 4506-T Forms: We require all of our loan officers to get pages one and two of the individual tax returns for two years in order to allow us to properly address this item, so it will not get rejected.

These are just some of the most common examples of missing information I often see. The bottom line is that if the application from your consumer is complete, and you create a much smoother road for everyone to travel down, your loans will close with ease. We have enough hurdles placed in front of us with new regulations, so try not to create internal issues with incomplete loan applications.

Now the next question that comes up is where to send applications for mortgages. The first place to start is with your own personal sphere of influence. An easy exercise for you to do is to write down a hundred names of people you know that either have a connection to real estate or own their own property. The very first thing you do is, once you have your business cards ready, hand write personal notes to all one hundred individuals on this list to let them know you are in the industry. We will also cover the social media aspect of making your announcement, but, in my personal experience, a good handwritten note with your contact information is still the best way to get going. This helps you get started on two fronts: first, you are practicing building a list for marketing purposes, and second, you are making your first request for business with the announcement. Personally, I would choose a direct path and ask these one hundred people to connect you if they, or anyone they know, needs a mortgage. Once you complete your first one hundred, you can start on a second list of a hundred people, and keep going as large as you can go when you make your sphere of influence with personal contacts for friends and family.

You will also look to pick some of the niche marketing efforts we have covered in this book, and then apply the time-blocking game plan. In addition to the time blocking, I have created scorecards to help turn prospecting in to more of a game, and a tangible exercise where you can see one on a weekly, and then monthly, basis. Management can use this with you, and you can track your point totals. The scorecard is also about accountability.

Looking at the card, you can see that I have broken it down into activities that will result in a very productive pipeline. I have assigned values to each activity, and as you can see, the more contacts and positive activities you do, the higher your point total. You will want to hit a consistent number of a hundred per week or four hundred per month. I also advise you to remain honest with yourself. If you find it necessary to cheat the sheet, you're really only cheating yourself. If you do the work that adds up the point values, you will see positive results. What the score card allows you to do with sales is to quantify your daily activity to create consistency for sales production.

There are many solutions to achieving success in our industry, and these methods may seem simple, but the key is to replicate them over and over again to achieve your desired results. With any type of sales, there are many ways to achieve success. However, these methods haven proven successful for myself, and loan officers I have trained over the last decade. The next page is an example of the scorecard we use:

Loan Officer Sales Calls Score Card
Points = Productivity

100 Points Weekly Goal
400 Points Monthly Goal

Name _____   Date _____

Point Type   **Point Value**   **Total**

Applications

Taken/closing: 10, 10, 10, 10, 10, 10, 10, 10, 10, 10, 10, 10 = _____

Call (5 to 1 pt): 1 1 1 1 1 1 1 1 1 1 1 1 1 1 1 1 1 1 1 1 1 1 1 1 = _____

1 1 1 1 1 1 1 1 1 1 1 1 1 1 1 1 1 1 1 1 1 1 1 1 = _____

1 1 1 1 1 1 1 1 1 1 1 1 1 1 1 1 1 1 1 1 1 1 1 1 = _____

Insurance Referral: 2 2 2 2 2 2 2 2 2 2 2 2 2 2 2 2 2 2 2 2 2 2 = _____

New Referral Source: 3 3 3 3 3 3 3 3 3 3 3 3 3 3 3 3 3 3 3 3 3 = _____

Sell a Bi weekly: 5 5 5 5 5 5 5 5 5 5 5 5 5 5 5 5 5 5 5 5 5 5 5 = _____

Referral: 10, 10, 10, 10, 10, 10, 10, 10, 10, 10, 10, 10, 10   = _____

SCORECARD TOTAL   _____

X_____   **Date** _____

Agent Signature   Scorecard due each
Friday afternoon

4

Directly Mailing Pieces to Top Agents

A LOAN OFFICER THAT is either new to a market, or looking to grow his or her business, can use a niche-market mailing approach. This is an example of a mailing campaign I did for 2016, and I will include copies of the mailers I used with a structured approach. I am doing this in an effort to gain business from the top realtors in my market. A new loan officer could use this same technique to get new business, as well as a loan officer relocating to a new market.

For my campaign I used a niche-specific approach. As a broker, we have some options that may or may not exist at local, regional, or national banks. I am going to use this to my advantage, and set myself up as an expert for difficult loans. I use this approach with the top realtors, because, for the most part, they are going to have some key lenders they already use. I am using the approach based on them wanting to send me something that may not get done by their normal lenders to let me take a look. By focusing your efforts on the top-volume producers in your area, you should pick up some deals from each of them that allow you to get your foot in the door. The next step will be up to you, to see if you mesh well with that realtor, or if they have issues with their current lenders. By setting yourself apart from the other lenders, you will potentially open doors.

A few quick pointers on the set up of how to go about creating mailing for targeting prospects with mail pieces. The first pointer is that you need to hand write your addresses. You have a higher chance of someone opening a handwritten envelope versus a printed or mass-mailed piece. I also use stamps and a generic envelope (old standard number ten, self-adhesive). I can't stress enough that the personal touch of taking this time, gives you a better chance of your message being opened and received. You also want to use neat handwriting, and take your time. On the trifold flyers you will see that we have the return address and place stamp on the back side so they are ready to be printed and stamped. One simple item to also make sure of is to get self-adhesive envelopes so you don't have to lick or wet the back of the envelope. A higher quality of printed paper is also recommended. I would go with a semi- or true glossy piece. These little extra touches will make your mail stand out in a pile of mass-mailed items. You also want to mail directly to your realtors' business address. At the same time you are doing your mailing, you need to create a detailed spreadsheet so you can follow up on your mailings, and have their contact information in place—both e-mail and phone. It will take time to build your list, but that will also let you appreciate the effort you are placing into this marketing. It is important that your efforts be complete, and that means making the follow-up call to contact to your mailing pieces. One other item is to make sure to spell check your marketing items, and proof-read them prior to printing. Speaking from experience, it is not cheap to reprint several hundred color prints. Take your time setting up your mailing, and take your time producing the finished product. This is an extension of your brand and your name.

It is also important to make sure you build a good target list, and that you have good contact information. The best way to handle this is to get a list directly from a realtors MLS system, or you can do this via Google, and put them into your spreadsheet. Make sure you spell their names correctly.

The key component here is that we have a system in place to keep putting your name in front of the realtors. I am going to use a mailing campaign combined with a quarterly event. In my market, we have a slightly older generation of realtors, so they are still very used to getting and receiving mail. If you are approaching a more tech-oriented group, you may have to change your approach or you will miss your mark. This would be more along the lines of e-mail. I will warn you though, that in our current market, people get a lot of e-mails, and it is very easy to find yourself in the junk mailbox. I plan to combine a regular meet-and-greet event at local restaurants and bars in a happy-hour format. A loan officer that is starting out may not be able to budget for this type of event, but I can assure you that these types of face-to-face events are a necessity. We will go over hosting events in later chapters. In my market, I am able to get my investor who's offering these products to attend the events with me, which is a big plus. In either case, whether you are sending direct mail or e-mails, you absolutely have to follow up a mailing or e-mail blast with phone calls. We will also develop a few scripts in this chapter based upon a few different types of calls. In this mailing, I'm going to approach all of these realtors with a very simple message that I will repeat over and over again: "Send me your difficult loans" or "Let's see what options I may have to help you sell another house."

This approach is really a strong way to get your foot in the door with new realtor prospects. Sure their bank can do that 780 credit score with 20 percent down, but do they offer a bank statement program? Do they have programs for borrowers with recent derogatory mortgage events, like a short sale or foreclosure? That answer in the 2016 market place is most likely not. Given that banks want to securitize as many of their loans as possible via Fannie and Freddie, they are not going to focus on these niche products. A broker needs to be synonymous with offering more options to these realtors.

Starting in January of 2016, I am going to send out the following information to the top two hundred realtors in my market once a month. I'm then going to follow up with a simple call and a simple message. I am going to set my calendar so I have my mailing ready to go between the 1st and 5th of each month. You will also want to create a spreadsheet with the realtor's name, address, and company name, and spots to mark off each mailing. All flyers will be in the appendix in order. Event mailing will go out the first of the month with a date for the end of the month at a local restaurant or bar with a request for RSVP.

January	Tri-fold Mailer
February	Summary-of-Options Flyer
March	Niche Bank Statement Program
April	Event Mailing
May	Niche Investor Cash Flow
June	Niche Recent Housing Event
July	Event Mailing
August	Niche Credit Score for Jumbo
September	Niche Construction Rehab Loan
October	Event Mailing

| November | Summary of Options Flyer |
| December | Happy Holidays Post Card |

After each mailing, you should spend the following week doing follow-up calls. Keep in mind, these are going to be business people, but you need to get them on the phone so you can get your message across. Once you have made contact, ask if it is acceptable for them to add you to an e-mail list so they have your contact information. You will most likely be told that they already have a lender or banker. Your response to this is very simple: "I understand that, and I just want to present myself as an option for a difficult deal they may not be able to get done for you. Please take a look at the options we have available for your buyers. My goal is to help you sell one more home per month."

This message really is universal, whether you are a ten-year veteran in the industry, or a newer loan officer starting out. You want to present yourself as a resource, not a pesky lender asking for business. The marketing material is key, because it gets the message across that you have options. Realtors closing a lot of business will have existing relationships. You do not want to approach them as the guy trying to change their way of doing business. Instead, you want to clearly be an option or a tool they can turn to when they have a difficult deal. Plain and simple, you have to put some performance in before you can earn their business.

This is a very basic drip campaign that can be used anywhere by anyone. Getting the list of realtors is also very simple. You can either get a realtor partner to print out a stats list for your area, or you can look within the local community for their awards. I am using the realtor-of-distinction winners for my area as my base list for mailings.

When hosting events, it is always important to remember your audience. Typically, we are going to be hosting events for realtors or referral partners. You can also have events for past clients, but I will be honest with you: given where and how much business you do in various areas, it may be very hard to get past clients to come to an event. This is because, for the most part, they will be in a satisfactory mortgage already, and if you are going to contact them it would be for a refinance opportunity.

Let's focus this effort strictly on our realtors and referral partners. There are several key factors to take in to account prior to your event. You need to set this up as a professional gathering, and in most cases that involves a restaurant or bar for either lunch or happy hour. You can change the type of your events based upon the number of your group.

In my market, we have a number of trendy restaurants and gathering spots, but I will warn you that it can get very expensive very quickly if you don't plan ahead. Let's start with your mailing. The mailing needs to clearly call for an RSVP so you're able to get an accurate head count. The mailing obviously needs to include the location, time, and basics of the gathering. I always offer a giveaway of some type, such as a trip to a hotel in the area for a weekend. This will help improve your response ratio. One key thing to remember is not to send an event mailing to group of cold contacts. In my case, I am focusing my efforts on the two hundred realtors we've identified as high-volume producers. I am also going to supplement my mailings to these realtors with event invites for everyone in their entire office. To get a good event turnout, you need to expand your numbers some, and just to be safe, I should expect to mail at least five hundred invites to an event. Also, I would always start with an event that has a social setting, such as a happy hour, first, and then try to organize a luncheon. I am also going to rely on my investor in this case, because my account representative is local. It is a good idea to rely on your account reps to key an event like this, because you can tie it back to the niche mailing you have already been doing as part of the direct-mail campaign.

Even before your mailing you need to decide on your venue. Your choice of venue is very important, because you want people to attend. The key factors I look for in a venue are whether it has an open area, if it's a trendy or newer location, whether it has a private space, and to make sure it's not too crowded. You do not necessarily want to go to a crowded venue that already has a lot going on. You want to be able to engage your group. You also want to be able to have the ability to pre-order food, and for there to be a semi-private to private area in which your group can socialize. Typically the best days of the week for a meeting of this nature are Wednesday or Thursday. I would never plan an event to happen on a weekend or early in the week, because you will not have good attendance. Depending on your market, Friday afternoon may be a good day of the week. It just depends on whether the members of your group members tend to stay in town or head out of town. Weather could be a factor when it comes to these types of events as well. In Charleston, we are blessed with a lot of open-air venues and sun. If you are in the northeast, or somewhere that tends to keep people indoors due to weather, then you will most likely have success with an event held on a Friday. In Charleston, it would be very difficult to get a group to attend on a Friday, as people are typically traveling, boating, or hitting the beach if the weather is nice. I would say that for places that have warmer climates, events should be held more mid-week as opposed to Fridays.

The thing to remember about hosting an event is that the event can feel like a success because of the amount of work that goes in to just hosting something with referral partners. Don't let that fool you. Your work is just beginning once the event has taken place. The only way an event is really a success is if it leads to more business for you. That means you have to follow up with the attendees, and be direct in asking for business. If you do not convert the event into future sales, then all you have done is spend money with no results. Results are what matters, so here are few keys points to consider after you've held your event.

14. Immediately follow up with attendees.
15. Ask for referrals or clients.
16. Put them in to your database for marketing purposes.
17. Schedule individual appointments with promising leads.
18. Set expectations.

The follow up is the most important part of making your event a success. It is a relationship-building process, but at the same time, you've got to convert these types of gatherings in to sales so that you can keep cash in the coffers to host more events. If you do not follow up with your attendees, and make doing so part of your business model, all you are doing is wasting your money.

If you are doing a nominal giveaway item, consider targeting it to your top candidates. If you are doing a live drawing during your event, then the winner will be chosen at random. However, there is nothing stopping you from offering something to the other attendees as well.

5

Credit Repair for
Your Clients

LET'S FACE IT, we are going to see as many bad credit scores as 720+ from those wanting to become borrowers, and in some cases this is a niche that many brokers are used to servicing. The reality is that, after the meltdown, many homeowners lost their property, dealt with short sales, and, in some cases, forced into bankruptcy. The good news for a seasoned mortgage broker is that the opportunity to advise someone on rebuilding credit exists, and it is a niche that can be very profitable that will allow you to build a loyal following.

The key to dealing with the credit-challenged, is that you have to help them set realistic goals and expectations. There are less cases that can be fixed overnight versus those that need a consistent rebuild prior to purchasing a home. Knowing some items that will help your consumers get credit, or improve lagging scores, will be the difference in several deals a month. Most banks will have higher credit score limitations, and almost all banks I deal with do not allow for a re-scoring process. Instead, they go with the idea that once they pull a score, that is their snapshot in time of the consumer. This presents an opportunity for mortgage brokers, and knowing some easy pointers will help you get, and ultimately close, more deals.

Let's break down the types of clients down into several classifications, and then look at each group. Each group represents different hurdles and challenges.

19. New Buyers with Thin Credit
20. Bad Credit, No Major Past Mortgage Events
21. Past Mortgage Events (Short Sale; Deed in lieu; Foreclosure)
22. Bankruptcy Clients

The easiest group to work with will be new buyers with thin, or marginally bad, credit. Typically these buyers have some bad items like collection accounts, little-to-no revolving trade lines, maybe student loan debt, and possibly some public records. This type of buyer often times are first-time homebuyers with very little in the way of active trade lines. A trade line is simply credit extended by a creditor. With a "thin-credit client," they often times do not have any of the three major trade lines we see with mortgages, installment loans, or revolving lines of credit. Mortgages are the most important trade lines, or type of credit, a consumer can have. With this type of consumer, they'll most likely be looking at their first purchase, and won't have a mortgage trade line to report. The next type of credit is an installment loan, and consists of a fixed payment made within a specific time period, typically once every thirty days. Installment loans include car payments, student loans, furniture contracts, and sometimes consumer advance loans. The most common type of installment loan you will see with first-time home buyers is either student loans or car payments. The final type of debt or trade line involves revolving accounts or credit cards. With thin-credit situations, typically you are missing several types of trade lines. Since we know the mortgage is one of the trade lines they are missing, you often times see a second type of credit missing in addition to a mortgage trade line, thus why the person has little-to-no established credit.

A simple solution for a thin-credit situation is a secured credit card. This type of card is offered at basically all major banks, including Bank of America and Wells Fargo, and allows the consumer to put down a deposit on their line of credit. The card type is guaranteed, because they get a line of credit equal to the amount of money they have put down. All of these types of cards will include a servicing fee of some type paid to the bank, but they are a quick and effective way to establish some revolving credit for your consumer. This type of consumer does take some hand holding, and will require some effort in terms of how much you'll need to work with them while they build up the scores.

Gas cards are also pretty easy for the consumer to obtain because they typically will have lower credit limits. Some banks may also offer overdraft protection as a trade line, but I have noticed they are getting away from that practice in lieu of just issuing credit cards at higher rates to the consumer.

If you see items that need to be cleaned up, like tax liens or collections, obviously those need to be addressed at the same time you are working with them to get the consumer's scores up. Older collections may not have as much of an effect on the scoring, depending on how long ago the collection occurred. The more recent the event, the more damaging it can be on their score.

Another key with these first-time buyers, is that they do not need to have everyone in town pulling their credit in attempts to issue them credit. The number of pulls will impact them negatively. One thing you can also see on all credit reports is who else is pulling their credit. Make sure you are keeping tabs on who else is involved in the process, including any other potential lenders, or multiple pulls that signal the consumer is over-extending themselves.

Typically with a credit-builder client, you will be focused in on FHA, VA, or USDA lending, as they will not have the scores to obtain conventional financing yet, or the mortgage insurance required for lower down payments.

The second main type of client—and potentially the most time consuming—are the clients with bad credit, but no major mortgage events. This type of client is going to have past late payments, collections, public records, and issues in general. These clients are going to have to do major work by themselves, or work with a credit repair agency in some cases. With these types of major issues, I only want to advise from a broker's perspective as far as what you need to watch out for that could act as potential deal killers, or non-starters.

The most important aspect to these clients is whether there is an issue that cannot be overcome to allow them to get them a home loan. The deal killers are going to be judgments that can't be paid off, tax liens, and collections over five thousand dollars that the borrowers do not have sufficient assets to pay off. These clients will not have had past mortgage events, but do face a number of challenges. As the broker, you want to make sure none of the deal killers are present, and if you have recent late payments, fees, etc., you need to weigh out what you really can do for the client.

Most lower-end FHA lenders will have a 580 cut off, and the 580 to 620 window is a tight window in terms of what they will allow and what will allow them to give you an approval. Getting over 620 will improve your chances of getting a deal done for these consumers. The consumers with past bad credit will need to look to achieve at least a 580, and depending on the depth of the past bad issues, you may be better advised to get to a 620.

Telling someone with past bad credit issues what to do is only part of the challenge. I typically take the approach of running the credit analyzer on our credit reporting system, and then afterward I'm more hands off. Either the client will do the work and take the steps to improve their credit, or they will not, but I do not want to spend a lot of time working with them if they do not show the desire to help themselves. In my state, you cannot act as a credit repair person and a broker, so we do not actively work with any consumer as they go through the actual steps to do the work. Instead, we provide a copy of the report for them, and let them either do the work and come back to us, or we assign them to a realtor for follow up. A loan officer really should not walk the line of trying to do major credit repair, and in some cases the steps credit repair companies take actually hurt us when we try to get a loan, since you can no longer have disputed items on a credit profile to get a Fannie Mae approval. My advice to any loan officer with a client that has past major credit issues is to give them some guidance, but do not spend too much time hand holding. These clients have had credit extended to them in the past, and have not used it wisely. I would think, given my experience with borrowers with past major items, that maybe two out of ten people will end up doing the necessary steps to get a home loan.

A slightly different classification is going to be a borrower that has had a past major mortgage event. These types of borrowers will primarily be looking at niche products that will require a large down payment. Most of these borrowers have owned a home in the past and know the advantages, and most likely were either affected by a short sale or foreclosure. Either type will have a seven-year hold to receive a conventional loan. The good news is that homeowners who were affected by the meltdown back in 2008 are just getting ready to start passing that threshold, which will make them eligible for home loans through more traditional means. The niche products will require much more skin in the game for a second chance after a major mortgage event. If they have the down payment, and have rebuilt their credit some, then there is most likely a loan out there for them.

A final classification of credit-challenged clients, are those clients who are coming out of bankruptcy. FHA and niche lenders are going to be the primary methods required to get these consumers back in to home loans. The type of bankruptcy will affect what they are able to do, whether it be a chapter thirteen or a chapter seven. Just for a basic purposes of understanding, a chapter thirteen BK means they did try to repay their debts at a reduced amount or interest rate. A chapter seven BK means they did not attempt to pay anyone back. One underlying factor with bankruptcy clients is whether or not the home was included in the bankruptcy. You will need to be able to review their bankruptcy pay history, and schedule inventory to make that determination.

The general rule to keep in mind with all credit-challenged clients is where there's a will, there is usually a way. If someone is willing to work to either build or improve their credit, then I tend to find them to be a worthwhile consumer to get in to a home loan. Clients with past major events may have fallen down, but also deserve a chance to get back up and purchase their own piece of the American dream. Their cost to play the game the second time is generally much higher, and it will require more money on their part, but, again, getting them a home loan can be accomplished.

SECTION 2:

Sales Innovations
and Techniques

Our middle section will focus on new and innovative ideas coming to the marketplace for mortgage professionals. These marketing companies, in most cases, will be ready to help you grow your business immediately, as we are covering innovation that is out there right now. You will also be able to find these and other products that will help you close more loans in my weekly newsletter, and you can register for the Weekly Sales Approach to Mortgage on my website at www.jasoncmyers.com.

Hometrackr is a mortgage lead company founded in October 2013 by Rich Estes, and can be found online at www.homtrackr.com. A couple of quick disclaimers: I have known Rich for many years, and he is actually a fraternity brother of mine. He got his initial introduction in to the world of real estate as a homebuilder, and then took time to get his MBA prior to founding Hometrackr. I have worked with him almost from day one when he first launched his company, and I am familiar with their products, so I have seen and worked with him through several changes made within his business model from its original state to its current form in 2016.

Let's start with what they provide and how they initially came to the market place. The basic concept of a Hometrackr report is a "Car Fax for Homes," and initially that is exactly what their product offering targeted for every consumer. Hometrackr taps into data for permits, contractors, and public records for a specific address, and gives a home history report similar to a home inspection, but with details on the history of where the property has been in terms of any repairs, upgrades, etc. Initially, the plan was to sell the report directly to the consumer for a nominal price, but that plan has changed, and has now evolved into a lead-based application with social media features.

Hometrackr now gives away the report in the forms of credits purchased by industry professionals. The lead is actually a format that is of value not only to a mortgage professional, but to realtors, insurance agents, and contractors as well. The report itself is branded to the professional, specific to addresses of interest, and can be pulled on any property in any state.

At first, a mortgage professional may say, "How does a home history report help me?"

Well the simple answer is that, directly, it may or may not be of value to the professional, but the real value is that the report will help you build relationships with clients and realtors through the numerous other applications. The report itself is typically of value to someone who falls into one of three categories: the homeowner, a potential buyer, or a homeowner looking to possibly sell their property. Hometrackr actually has screening windows that test for the validity of the contact information, as well as filters to screen out the window shoppers. What this allows is for you to only spend your money on people that fall into designated categories, including people interested in buying a property or listing one for sale.

Each lead can be customized to achieve these goals for the loan officer. One word of warning: the more you attempt to screen the lead upfront, the bigger turn off this can be to the consumer. You may screen your way out of potential deals. Hometrackr recommends that you only do one potential additional screen after the initial contact information. They get information to confirm you have a good e-mail address and phone number for each lead.

Let's explain how this works for the mortgage professional. Your company pays a one-time, nominal set-up fee with a very reasonable amount required for ongoing access to reports. The monthly fee is paid per user, and gives the user access to the reports.

Now here is where it gets cool and fun. Part of the service is that Hometrackr will manage your account to three social media outlets. You get to pick from Linkedin, Facebook, Twitter, Instagram, e-mail blast, and Google plus. At the time of writing this book, they are also working on a text-messaging feature for marketing. So, as part of your package, they will get ads out for you to give away free reports via social media, which is the most effective platform, and pretty much a must-have, because Facebook is the most successful application. For the social-media-inept loan officer, you can get in the social media pool and have someone manage giving away a product that will give you potential sales. The exclusive lead campaign is the cool part of the application which will include Widgets and ad management that gives you a push into active social media. As people access and take advantage of your free offer, then you get leads to use with either realtor partners or even potential home buyers.

The lead itself is also something that can be farmed out, and shared with other referral partners. An enterprising loan officer now has something of value to give to potential listing agents, as well as contractors and insurance agents. Keep in mind, the lead itself belongs to you if it comes from your social media platform. Hometrackr is also doing their own marketing to create leads to sell to the same groups of potential end users. You could split the cost with other partners to lower your overall costs.

Why use this type of lead? In comparison, the cost of roughly ninety-nine dollars per user at the time of this writing is very cost effective to create leads and get a social media presence. The ninety-nine-dollar package gives the user ten reports to give out to clients or via social media. There are packages that allow for more units, and if you have a month where you give out less, you keep the ones you did not give out as credits for future months, just like rollover minutes. The lead itself is not always a red-hot buyer who's ready to go, so you do have to have some initiative to get value from the lead by having partners lined up to hand off potential listings, and other partners who could benefit, including insurance agents and contractors.

The lead itself is also compatible with all client-management systems, and it can be loaded into your marketing campaigns. The lead is also owned by the loan officer, and can be referred to any referral partner. A joint marketing agreement with realtors, contractors, or insurance agents is also allowed, so you could defer some of your costs.

So here is the innovative part of this lead system: you get to set up your screens, and get an actively managed social media campaign for a fraction of the cost associated with other lead programs. It will give you the ability to create leads to give out to your referral partners. It is always best to give a lead before asking for a lead in return. You are also partnering with a company that is creating a tangible item that is branded to you and your company. Hometrackr is also actively in the process of adding quality rating systems, like Guild Quality and Enerscore.

Just to touch briefly on these two ideas: Enerscore is currently trying to create a rating system for homes based upon the type and quality of their energy consumption. So think of it like this: there are two homes in the same neighborhood, but one home may have a higher enerscore rating due to newer appliances, newer cooling systems, and quality of construction. Guild Quality is also working on a similar rating for the quality of construction of home builders so that a rating system exists for how well built a home is, and it can be assigned online, and is available for consumers. All of these features come in the package for you as you begin to use and work the system.

For the loan officer this is a unique type of lead, but let me also caution you that this not the type of lead that you just call until they decide to refinance with you. These really are not that type of lead. While you can get deals, I think these leads lend themselves more to helping you build relationships with realtors and other partners. I would consider partnering directly with an insurance agent, and even a contractor, to offset some of the costs. Keep yourself flexible with the realtor you assign the leads to, because you could be receiving listings from various areas, which gives you the opportunity to farm out the leads to different agents.

Overall, the type of lead structure given to you by Hometrackr is unique in today's marketplace, and it will be a different style of lead from what the average loan officer is used to working with. If you do not put in effort to networking the lead to partners, you may not see success with this type of lead. These are not quick-and-easy refinance leads, so you need to plan ahead to see good results.

6

Originator IQ or AAN

T HE NEXT GROUP is a type of service that can be used in conjunction with Hometrackr, and requires the loan officers to commit to various styles of purchase-driven lead sources. Originator IQ is a unique service provider that attempts to match a loan officer's pre-approved buyers with high-volume listing agent teams that also have buyers' agents working on them. There a contractual protection component that makes their service unique to the industry, and can be a benefit to mortgage brokers who can produce high amounts of pre-approved buyers through their own means.

Let's take a look at a typical issue associated with working purchase leads, and the solution that is provided by Originator IQ will become more obvious and seem more unique. Looking at just the costs dynamic of an Internet purchase lead versus an Internet refinance lead, the first and most obvious difference is that refinance leads, on average, cost three times as much as purchase leads. One might ask why? The main issue when doing purchase transactions is that with any amount of volume, you have a harder time pinning down the geographic area for your buyers.

This simple example will illustrate the main issue. If you buy purchase leads from Lending Tree, for example, they can't guarantee how close the purchase lead will actually be to your location. So for the state of South Carolina, we have a geographic area that could create leads all over the state. We do not have the compact urban area that some major cities have, and this leads to geographic hurdles. Most realtors are registered in certain geographic areas. In Charleston, for example, they are part of the Tri County CTAR, or a three-county region. A realtor in this market does not necessarily have the same level of access to the multiple listing service in another area, such as the Columbia market. That is a completely different area with different computer operating software and licensing costs. Just to keep it simple, what realtor is going to want to drive over an hour and a half away to try to show a $200,000 house? Pretty much none of the ones I work with are going to be able, or willing, to commit to this type of transaction. So what these Internet leads allow you to get purchase transactions that could be anywhere in the state. Even with a vast network of realtors, it would create some unique logistical issues, especially if you get a pre-approved buyer in an area where you have to find a realtor just to show property. This leads to the second issue for the loan officer, which is cost—the cost associated with issuing that pre-approval, including the lead cost itself and credit report fees, not to mention the opportunity cost that comes with spending time on the phone with the client, and finding a potential realtor to help your client.

Any number of variables can lead to this type of scenario not translating into dollars for the mortgage professional. I have run a large-scale call center, and we did operate using purchase leads, and I would say our success ratio with getting loans closed after pre-approval was somewhere between the 15 to 20 percent range, which is not very good overall. There are a lot of potential deal killers for you, including local competition, builders preferred lenders, potential realtor conflicts, and whether the buyer finds what they want in that market. Also, in most cases, if you are dealing with buyers out of your market, you are not able to meet with them face to face, which would allow you to build the rapport necessary to make them a solid client. We tried many methods, including Skype, that would allow face-to-face interaction, but the results still lagged behind our in-market purchase transactions with dramatic numbers. We were able to close a pre-approval done in person in our market with solid realtor partners 85 percent of the time. We very rarely lost a client to another competitor. The main issues we saw involved people who had run into credit issues after a pre-approval, people with inspection issues, or those who had just plain lost interest.

Let's fast forward to how Originator IQ comes into the equation, and what they potentially offer to a loan officer.

7

Sales Techniques:

Hard Money and Commercial Deals

A S A BROKER, you will have the opportunity to add some more control to your product offering, including some hard-money options and commercial. Both options can add additional income to your business. Let's break down each one, and in getting started with both a good source to find potential lending partners is the Scotsman Guide. The resource section will give you points of contact so you can sign up with them as a broker. These types of loans will fall under Dodd Frank, and require compensation plans and disclosure on settlement statements.

Adding in Hard Money is a natural action for a broker to take to give options to borrowers that do not fit inside any of your lending-option boxes. Hard money essentially means non-traditional financing, and can be for borrowers that have some form of limitation. Examples of limitations may be past mortgage events, income underwriting issues, unique property types, past credit issues, and basically anything that makes it difficult for a borrower to obtain normal or traditional financing. Before you go the route of hard money, make sure you have gone to all possible conforming and niche products there are available. You have to make sure the hard-money route is the only option the client has left, and that it fits the needs of the client. Hard-money lending is not for every client.

Typically hard money deals will include higher rates, prepaid interest, very low loan to values, and higher origination costs. You have to ask whether this type of loan is appropriate for your client. Hard-money lending is usually done for clients that have past experience with loans, and may have had some difficulty with credit issues in the past. That's not to say that all the clients will have bad credit, but this is a type of lending is for people who have past issues. Keep in mind that rates will be determined by state regulations and rules, and the investor will have to be in compliance, and have a state license to lend in your home state.

Hard money, or non-traditional financing, can also be necessary for distress property types, or for unique properties. Examples where a consumer might need non-traditional financing would be for condo conversion, condotels, mixed-use property, apartment complexes, and property in disrepair. Condos can be an example of a property type that could need some non-traditional options. Condos may have issues with their HOAs, like high investor concentration, insurance coverage problems, and litigation. Condotels are also a property type that, as of 2016, have not regained popularity. There are some niche lenders that are now doing Condotels, including Angel Oak, but they are very selective with the project. Hard money may be the only option to get these types of deals done.

Land loans, or lot loans, are another example of property that may need non-traditional financing. Banks are pushing more for the construction loan portion of any involvement to do land financing. This is from past experience, when land or lot loans went bad after 2008. Instead, they prefer to have a construction loan in process so there is structure in case of the need for future foreclosure. That being said, this presents an opportunity for a broker to offer lot loans via non-traditional financing lenders. Borrowers will need to expect larger down payments and higher rates, but they will also get financing terms on property types that are not in favor right now with traditional banks.

The main factor you need to keep in mind with non-traditional financing, is that it is not appropriate for every single borrower, but it is a subsection of the lending market today that can't be ignored. A good broker will add this tool to the tool box so that they always have the potential to make another deal happen for your consumer.

Be certain that you disclose a hard-money deal just like any other deal, and that your licensing is in order, and you have broker approval with your lender. Hard-money lending is really no different than working with any of your other lenders. Commercial lending will involve businesses or LLCs instead of your normal consumers, and will typically involve much larger loan sizes. A typical commercial deal will be in excess of $500,000, all the way up to $10 million. Commercial lending has an appeal just based on those numbers alone.

Commercial lending is an offshoot of the same concept of non-traditional financing options for your clients. Commercial lending will be different from hard money, so don't confuse the two options. Commercial lending does have some different issues you need to weigh out as part of your business plan. My first, and most important, piece of advice for any broker looking to do commercial is to understand your client and the situation. As a commercial broker, you need to have a very solid source of lending, and to understand their product matrix. I do not recommend dipping a toe into commercial lending for anyone who has been in the business less than ten years. The main reason is that commercial lending requires a lot of work, and if you are in a competitive situation you can lose deals after you put a lot of time and effort in to the process.

If you set up with most commercial lenders, they will give you an idea of what they will require as upfront fees for consumers. Most commercial brokers will require up-front commitments as a part of a term-sheet offer to the consumer. The reason for this is to create some skin in the game for the consumer. The reason most commercial brokers that this step is that in a competitive situation with banks, they are often at a disadvantage. A commercial bank has other items like banking, credit services, credit card processing, depository relationships, and other banking services they can offer to a client. A commercial broker is basically just offering loan terms. A bank that is aggressively in a deal with you can offer trade-offs on other banking services that a commercial broker will not bring to the table. I have been in situations before where I was competing with a bank, only to have them use our term sheet and match the rates to keep the client. This can be a very frustrating issue, and can be a major turn off to any mortgage broker looking to do commercial deals.

That being said, I have taken the step to set up a relationship with a commercial broker who we just use for direct referral business. This way, we do not spend much of the time and effort in working the loan. We also are limited on what we make—typically a hundred to two hundred basis points—but at least we have the option without a lot of the headache. This gives me options to refer in potential commercial clients, but not spend time working those that aren't part of my core business. I would strongly recommend that you approach commercial business the same way. Again, the Scotsman Guide can give a number of commercial outlets, and you can find the right match for you.

A word of warning: You need to be very, very clear with your client that commercial is not your primary business. You also need to properly disclose in writing any fees you will receive should a deal go through. Again, you also need to see if the commercial broker requires an investor package prior to doing business together, and any type of disclosure you need regarding the fees they charge to the consumer. Unlike traditional consumer business, commercial business is typically done with businesses. This changes the requirements, as this is no longer a residential home loan. For lack of a better explanation, the government assumes that everyone doing business with commercial deals are big boys, and they know what they are signing up for in advance of doing deals together.

The main things you need to watch out for are that the commercial outlet you are using has a good reputation, and the ability to deliver on term sheets. Typically with my referral source, I am only involved until the term sheet is issued and fees disclosed. At that point, I take a step back and let the commercial broker handle everything, and I do a conference call hand-off with the client to explain that I am now no longer involved in setting up the deal. This is important, because you need to set the expectations for the clients regarding what comes next, and who will be handling the transaction.

There have been some commercial brokers that took deposit money with no intention of delivering on term sheets. We ran into this in several deals in Florida, and I recommend that if you do not know the commercial lender personally, that any contemplated deal should involve a third-party escrow agent, namely an attorney to hold the upfront money. The upfront money should also just be the fee to the commercial broker (including your fee), and does not include the fees associated with the underwriting of the deal, like appraisals, inspections, and legal work, all of which are typically handled separately. You could also have larger items like zoning, environmental issues, and design work that are not a part of the lending process, but part of the due diligence work that any customer should expect, which should most likely be handled before the financing begins for you.

Commercial is a different animal, so unless you want to just focus on commercial lending as your primary lending business, I suggest you follow the same approach that I take, which is to set up a simple referral relationship. Commercial has a lot of moving parts, and the loan sizes can be very large, but at the same time this also means there will be other people interested in the deals as well. I equate commercial lending to big game fishing. It is very nice when you land that Blue Marlin, but there are many days that pass in between catching that big fish. Anyone who has gone big-game fishing knows that you have to be patient, but you also have to use different methods—and it can mean you will only catch one big fish, or nothing at all. In our business, we have to keep catching fish to eat, so don't lose sight of the fish you can catch every day waiting for that big fish to come in.

Sales Tip for Existing Brokers

D on't forget about your withdrawn, or turned down, clients from the previous year. As a current broker, we have many past clients who, for whatever reason, do not end up closing, whether it was due to an issue with closing cost, credit mishap, or the client just got cold. There are past clients sitting in your database right now that could be deals in today's market.

The loan scenario and credit situations could change for the consumer at any given time. You have withdrawn clients sitting in your system right now that could be deals just a year later. I recommend that a more seasoned broker make these types of calls back through old deals that, for whatever reason, did not close. Give them calls just to update them, and check in with them.

You can also use a method to send them direct e-mails (not mass produced), and ask if they are interested in revisiting a loan at this time. If you have a rate dip, this process can be especially useful, as it keeps the client informed, and gives you the opportunity to sell them a deal. I have a more senior loan officer that does these types of calls usually starting the first of the following year. So he takes all of our withdrawn clients, or anyone who was denied from the previous year, and begins his attempts to reach out the clients to see if they have any interest.

So far, in 2016, he's had success with this method, so much so that I thought it worthwhile to mention in the new book. Each loan officer will have deals that get off track. Don't forget about these clients. Give them a call each year, and you should be satisfied with the result. Think of it like this to motivate yourself: You have already spent time and money in most cases when you've worked with those past withdrawn clients. Challenge yourself to capitalize on your money that's already been spent. Just by picking up one of those past loans that didn't close off the scrap heap each month, you will improve your bottom line in the long run.

These clients are just sitting in your existing book of business, so pick up the phone and give them a call!

9

Marketing Service Agreements

AGREEMENTS BETWEEN MORTGAGE brokers and realtors have been coming under further examination by the CFPB and local regulators in our industry—and this does not even get in to the potential litigation that is out there for these agreements. That covers the bad news, so now let's look at the right way to do MSAs, so that you can stay out of trouble, and in business with good partners. MSAs have been growing in popularity as a way to get business through joint marketing efforts by referral partners. The only issue is they are not being used properly in most cases I've seen.

To keep it simple, you can only pay for the marketing that you are getting, and the cost associated with that marketing. For example, let's use a billboard. If you and a realtor buy a billboard together, and your logo takes up

25 percent of the billboard and the realtor's takes up 75 percent of the billboard, then you are required to only pay for 25 percent of the cost of this billboard. Sound complicated? Well, it can be, and it can open up a can of worms you don't necessarily want to entertain, which could involve spending a lot of your money to support marketing efforts that may not work for you. It also opens up the possibility that you are being used to support a realtor's efforts that may or may not end up in business for you. I have seen many attempts at marketing with realtors that just plain do not fit the requirements under RESPA, and do not ultimately generate business.

The first thing about any MSA is that it needs to be written and authorized by both parties. RESPA rules require that mortgage brokers pay for their portion of marketing, and that it be a fixed amount based upon this written agreement. You can't tie an MSA to a number of transactions or to percentages. That is illegal, and something to watch out for when setting up a marketing agreement. One key item to look out for is whether you are replacing someone that was in the agreement prior to you, which is a warning sign that something did not work out before. My guess would be that the broker did not get what was expected, or the realtor did not get what they expected. The agreement thus should clearly spell out what each side expects, as well as spending on the marketing venture. I find it is best to start a marketing plan together with a realtor partner that did not previously exist. If you are picking up something that was a pre-existing marketing plan involving a loan officer before you, then that tells me it probably did not work out too well for the loan officer; otherwise, they would still be working it. Slots for successful business builders don't just open up. Building your own plan with a realtor as a true partner is the best way to go.

Let's use my own experience as examples of what works and what does not. As mentioned before, I took a boomtown site to one of my realtor partners, Scott Limehouse with Remax Southern Shores in Myrtle Beach, almost seven years ago, and we are still working on this project today, with both of us seeing the benefits. We split the costs 50/50, and we both work the leads. At this point in our careers, we have junior agents and brokers working the leads under us and with us. This is a relationship that works for us both, and it is compliant with all RESPA rules. Just this past fall of 2015, one of my junior loan officers came to me with an opportunity to get involved with a local reality team that does over $50 million a year in business. I was willing to support him, and we entered into an agreement for $1,000 a month provided that he receive leads at the same time. Well, four months go by, and we received no deals, which to me was an immediate red flag. Upon further investigation and further discussions with the head realtor, we determined that we were not getting what we paid for in terms of the business. Well, the first person to blame was myself, not my junior loan officer. I should have known, going into the transaction, that we were replacing another loan officer that was not a fit for this team of agents. I will say that we quickly figured out it was not working, and gracefully walked away from the deal.

Looking further at this failed experience, let's identify some potential warning signs I should have picked up on prior to entering into the MSA. For one, the type of business this team was doing was a 50/50 mix of listings to buyers. That means that half of their work was not really something that they could—or would—refer to us, but yet here we are paying for marketing that is of no benefit to us. The second warning sign should have been the fact that a lender was "in house" with their overall realty brokerage. They have one of the high-rent agreements in place with a regional mortgage broker. While we were told, of course, that they, as the realtor, refer their preferred lenders, you still have a problem that the competition has a geographic advantage being in the office where some of your potential clients come to meet with the agents you are supposedly paying for leads to work together. This problem is not a definite deal killer, but when you combine it with the fact you are replacing another lender, and that they have a second mortgage broker in place who's also paying a thousand dollars, I should have politely declined this deal upfront.

The non-exclusive splitting of fees is a huge red flag that I was honestly not aware of prior to agreeing to the MSA for my loan officer. I should have done further research, but let this be an example of the homework you need to do prior to entering into a marketing agreement. As a general rule, I will never again step into someone else's shoes on a deal involving marketing. I will either start the marketing plan from day one, or not participate at all. There is a lot of opportunity out there for building business. There is no reason to waste money on something that did not work for another mortgage broker. I equate this to seeing a restaurant fail, but yet you keep seeing new restaurants enter the same exact location in a shopping center, only to similarly fail later on. If it did not work for one broker, it is probably not going to work for you either, no matter the reason.

One option for MSAs—that is both compliant and works for both parties—is to use the Internet via search engine optimization to generate your leads. The cost of the lead can be split with the , and I always recommend splitting it 50/50, as this will generate leads that can actually be worked by both the mortgage broker and the realtor. This will help keep you compliant, as what you have paid for belongs to both of you. You have the same opportunity to work the lead as the realtor has. In some cases, you will get a deal that the realtor may not get, and vice versa. Working the deals together is the key. If you do not make the effort to call your leads, that is your own loss. Working the leads with your realtor is the best way to get the results you are paying for, but also the way to stay compliant under the law.

In my opinion, I would stay away from other marketing sources that do not generate a tangible lead for you. There is a lot of opportunity for you to waste money on items a realtor may want to have that just don't benefit you, the broker, and may open you up to all kinds of violations. I think that larger-scale marketing agreements and in-house lending services with big "rental" agreements will come under further examination, and could lead to big problems for lenders and realtors. Really, if you think about it, why should a lender be allowed to "rent" office space to be a preferred lender? What do the two have in common? I do not feel that in the long run these arrangements really work out for the two parties, and at the same time are going to result in potential fines and licensure issues. I can think of a few mortgage lenders who could face a number of issues with compliance down the road. I think it is best to win your business on merit and hard work. Market servicing agreements have their place if handled properly, but at the same time do not commit yourself to contracts that are not legal or not beneficial for both sides. I would not do any deals with realtors who you do not have a pre-existing relationship with, or with whom you've created a written marketing plan that has grown both of your brands. I think in the increasingly regulatory environment I would be very, very careful with the agreements you enter into, and make sure you are meeting all requirements for your state.

Most importantly, use the rule of common sense. If the costs are split mutually down the middle, and you get the same opportunity the realtor gets, then it is most likely a good deal for both sides. If you are just paying in to a top-of-mind awareness marketing so a realtor can be all over the place, then you may have issues with both costs and the legality of what you are doing. I think the lesson for all MSAs is to do it right from day one with a partner you can trust. Don't get pulled into agreements that seem too good to be true.

I would also keep an eye on these agreements, and update them with your clients each year, making sure that no new regulations from the state or CFPB come down that could affect how you are doing business. It is important to stay in front of any changes, because a lack to act on your part could result in fines.

10

Builder Business

I F YOUR MARKET is like ours, you have noticed that new construction is picking up, if not outright booming, at this point. New home builders, in my opinion, are their own type of referral source, because they have different needs for you to consider when you market to them. I focus my efforts on working with smaller regional or local builders, and I do not put as much focus on trying to get in with the national guys. Most national builders will have in-house services, or may have established larger scale MSAs. When focusing on the national builders, I focus solely on the site agents, and even their local in-house lender with our niche products that are most likely not offered by the builder-owned mortgage companies. For the most part I have found that they are very simple in their product offerings in an effort to lessen their risk, as well as being a way to solve the fact they don't have as much time to deal with the credit-challenged. Think about it logically. They do not want to risk building a $200,000 home for someone who needs credit repair. It puts way too much risk on them with a corporate business model. If the in-house lender and the site agent make a mistake tying up a home that eventually doesn't close, you can see where the hammer may fall, so to speak. Working with a national builder can also be a full-time gig if they really start to send you loans, but also keep in mind that you would be months away from paychecks as the homes get built.

I focus most of my efforts with my regional and local builders, because they seem to be a better fit with us from a size standpoint. They will most likely be sized, personnel-wise, similarly to your brokerage, and they will most likely be a small business owner just like you are going to be, so there is some basic levels of connection that are pre-existing. To gain a foothold, what I would suggest is to market to the owners specifically, and ask for the opportunity to be on their list. Be prepared that you will most likely get a harder deal before you see anything easy, and it may take a few no's to get to a yes in terms of getting a deal done.

When dealing with builders directly, you need to be upfront and always keep them in the loop. Don't be afraid to say no on some deals, because they are relying on your information to make decisions to build property. It just takes a few of your pre-approved buyers falling out for you to find yourself out of a preferred position with a builder.

Also keep in mind that these things happen, but that does mean that opportunity will come around, which I've seen, because most builders change their preferred lenders at least once a year. If you use an approach to pitch your niche products, you will get some shots at deals and be waiting in the wings when an opportunity comes your way.

Places to find the smaller builders are very easy to find. In our area, there is a publication specific to the new-home community, and a weekly new-home advertiser in the newspaper. Also, just get in the car, and drive around to the growing communities. They will all most likely have site agents, and there is your starting point to get an introduction. Another area you can look into involves people who are pulling permits. This can actually give you a leg up on your competition, because if you see a new builder to your area pulling permits, this will be in advance of them putting any work into the ground. and way in advance of if they are marketing. Another little nugget for you is that the building permit will typically have the builders name and address on it, so you can reach out and get in touch with them. This type of head start can be very important with a newer, regional, or start-up builder, because they may not be doing any advertising yet.

Planning ahead for your marketing is also a key component to doing business with builders. If you are not working onsite daily, then you will need to make sure you are leaving items behind that can be received by clients. Obviously business cards are one thing you will want to leave, but you will want to consider some other items as well. I have had success creating flyers for our new home communities in color with payment options. A lot of new home buyers are going to be comparing their current rental situation to the payment of a new home, so go ahead and put it out there. Make sure you are covering some basics by using the correct APR, and you will probably want a range of rates and product types. So if you are doing, say USDA, you will want to hit some of the highlights like 100 percent financing and the rate range. Typically over-estimate your rate by .25 percent to be safe, just so you don't have to reprint a ton of flyers all the time. You will also want to put a disclaimer to confirm the rate by calling you. Always get a vertical flyer holder so that the flyers will be more visible.

I also put up signage in every company that will allow it so that clients driving in over the weekend or at different times will be able to call you after hours. It also helps you to brand yourself to your builder. Make sure your signage is compliant with all state advertising rules. I would also make sure you have multiple points of contact, including e-mail, cell phone, and a website.

If you can attend regular sales meetings with your sales team, I would strongly suggest you go to the meetings.

Opportunity will present itself if loans being handled by other lenders run into problems. Being present is one of the most important aspects of being a preferred lender loan officer. You have to be around to be able to help them get more deals in the boat. The key with being a preferred lender is that you foster a positive relationship with your team ,and leave your marketing where it can be made readily available. Any loan officer can come drop off business cards—and to be compliant most builders/realtors will have multiple options listed—so you need to make sure your card or flyer is the one they reach for, and if you are fully involved in the sales and the community you should be the top choice over and over again.

You will also probably want to combine some form of open house when the weather permits in those model units. I have loan officers actually on-site at our model units several days a week. The open house can be something as simple as a drop in, but make sure you have something that allows you to capture information from the potential buyers and their agents as they come through the unit. You could consider giving away some type of prize each month, and leaving a fish bowl out for people to fill out information cards or drop business cards into for the realtors.

11

Rocket Mortgage

A s of writing this book, the "Rocket Mortgage" by Quicken has been generating both positive and negative news. Given their recent advertising campaign and commercials during the Super Bowl, some are asking if these types of loans will be a repeat of issues that almost crushed our economy. Personally, I think the Rocket Mortgage is innovative, but at the same time I ask this simple question: Is the vast majority of the general public going to want to have this process handled completely online with no human interaction? Is this going to eventually result in an issue of identity theft down the road for Quicken? I think if they get hit eventually with some type of security breach, or if they get hacked, it could be a major issue for them. I am sure they have put a lot of money, time, and research into those risks, but in today's society, it would not surprise me to see Quicken get attacked by hackers. Unfortunately, that is just a part of our world today. I think it just a matter of time before someone creates some type of scam designed to look like a Quicken Rocket Mortgage to obtain people's data. This is just my opinion, and I am sure Quicken has some form of security, but consumer confidence with this product is going to be a very unique component. People are used to putting their information out there, but this could also lead to a backlash if there is any type of widespread scam or security breach. Personally, I think the advertising and word of mouth chatter gets people thinking about brokers, and not retail banking, so I see this as a positive thing.

I see this type of lending as another niche that will appeal to some people, especially some of the millennial generation who are very tech savvy, and used to being online. I also think there will be people who simply are not confident in this type of lending who will stick to banks and brokers alike. I see this as an opportunity for mortgage brokers to once again pitch personal service. I think the majority of people will just not be ready to eliminate a loan officer in their lending decision. I also don't see how some of the credit-challenged individuals will find this to be a user-friendly system, because not everyone will fit into the Rocket Mortgage box. As of writing this book, the average credit score listed by Quicken for the Rocket Mortgage was a 754 middle score. That is certainly a smaller portion of home buyers, and does not represent everyone who will be applying.

I really think the people who will have the largest issue with the Rocket Mortgage, will be the realtors. I could see more issues with them not being able to be involved in the process, along with depending on an automated system for their paychecks. Most realtors I know have major issues just dealing with loan officers who aren't in their market, let alone an online application.

I will say I have not seen the rates associated with the Rocket Mortgage, or if it provides savings to the client, but I think this also just furthers my belief we'll all need the pricing flexibility to compete with these types of loans. I think that if all things are equal, the consumer will choose to work with a person locally over a computer or some type of service center.

I do think the advertising done by Quicken benefits us all, as they get the message out there, and for the most part are presenting mortgages as a positive thing. We need as many positive messages out there as possible after the meltdown. If the Rocket Mortgage gets people talking, and gets people looking at mortgage rates, I can only see that as a benefit for everyone in our industry.

I will say I wish them well, I just hope they don't do too well. I, for one, am not ready to be replaced by a robot. Just in case this happens, however, our next section may give you a good plan of attack for some of those credit pulls done by Quicken.

12

Trigger Leads

I F YOU ARE used to dealing with Internet leads, you've probably heard of "trigger" leads. If you wonder how your clients start receiving calls after you pull credit, then look no further than your friendly credit bureaus who are readily selling your borrowers information, which is known as a trigger lead.

A trigger lead is just that—a lead triggered by a mortgage credit pull. If you have filled out your loan application and included your borrowers cell phone or phone number, then that information is also passed along via the trigger lead. Here is a quick note: if you don't want your clients to get called, leave the contact information blank during the credit pull, and enter these details after you have pulled credit. With the move to cellular phones, for most consumers it will be much, much harder for anyone to track down your borrowers.

There are multiple places you can buy trigger lead data so you can get into that line of selling. Here are a few valid points: Typically with a trigger lead, you may be calling behind someone that was referred to the client. You will probably want to be able to compete with a very low rate, so I would recommend that anyone doing this type of prospecting look to have your warehouse line ready to go so you can name your own price. It would be harder to do a lot of this type of competition-driven business solely as a broker. I would really not recommend it, because you would not be able to go low to try and garner the business over the initial puller of the client's credit.

Also keep in mind that trigger lead data could also be sold by one of the other bureaus, so if you are getting trigger leads from an Experian-based source, there is nothing to say that another lender is not getting the same from Equifax.

Be prepared that you will have to fight to the end, and in a decreasing-rate environment, your rate locks could become issues. The loyalty of this type of client is often times suspect if they will move to you just based on rate. You have to get them closed efficiently, and be prepared to fight off the other potential lenders to the end. In some cases, you will also be spending money to buy leads when someone is working directly with a lender on a purchase. I would recommend if you are going to commit to this type of lead purchase that you focus on going behind some of the unique big lenders, like a Quicken Mortgage. If you have an option to buy the lead as an exclusive lead, by all means, I am a big proponent of being the only lender to buy the lead. In this case, you know at least one other player is sitting at the table trying to get the client's business, so you will want to limit any other potential lenders. One interesting technique I could see developing would be for people to ask for trigger-lead data specifically behind Quicken to counter the new Rocket Mortgage. Think about it. If someone is not 100 percent comfortable after the initial credit pull by Quicken with the Rocket Mortgage, an enterprising mortgage broker could come in with a personal touch, and call these clients. The broker could be a voice, and an offer of confidence, in a process that can be intimidating to some. If you can come in and offer a superior rate with superior customer service, you could very well garner business.

Also, in a sales case like this, don't get greedy. Just go as low as you can to get the deal, because this type of lending is a total volume play. You have to keep getting deals on the board to keep feeding the lead source. Happy hunting. I will say, this is not my favorite type of business to try and earn due to its low profitability and expense. I would not recommend this type of marketing, except to the most experienced loan officers with a superior back office system and their own warehouse line. Even if you don't do trigger leads, you need to be aware that they are out there, and you need to protect your files from them as much as possible when you can.

Internet leads in general are becoming harder to work, and keep this in mind: a lot of the larger companies doing Lending Tree, Zillow, and so forth, are all using Auto Dialers to get in touch with the clients. This puts a lot more pressure on the client. Similar to overfishing. Once a client puts their information out there for a potential purchase or refinance, we are seeing that lead get recycled over and over again by numerous sources. So even if they put their information just on one site, they will begin to get calls from other venders that were attached to that initial request. Even if you are paying for an exclusive lead the way I've recommended, there are other sources and other means by which other lenders are tracking down their information and potentially working your lead.

What this does is keep the profitability on these leads lower, and it means you have to maintain a high level of volume to make the system work. Internet leads are not bad, but they do mean you have to be fully committed to make this source of business work in the long run.

13

Crowd Funding

O NE MORE RECENT phenomenon that is out there is the concept of crowd-funding real estate property. There have been several new versions of this where people can put various amounts of money into specific projects. I think the idea here is to make some type of Frankenstein's monster of a REIT-meets-a-Hedge-fund-with-hard-money interest rates—one of those Internet sensations that seems too good to be true, and it probably isn't going to end well. I will not mention anyone specifically by name, but if you Google it they will pop up.

While I am all for the Internet making things available and providing information for all, this seems like a concept that is destined to end up badly for the investors. If you want to invest a thousand dollars into real estate, go buy a REIT mutual fund, but I would caution anyone looking at this as a way to make a living to not to quit your day job. The concept is very simple: the company setting up these deals is going to vet, or do some type of underwrite, on the borrower of the money. Let's be honest here: if someone is crowd funding a real estate deal, they may be unable to get financing traditionally, or they may be a novice at working on investment property. The big red flags I see involve setting specific time lines for the money to be returned to the investors, which is a concern, because if you know the real estate market, it is very hard to predict when a project will be both completed and sell for the dollars necessary to pay back the loan—plus whatever return the developer is going to be seeking. This also seems like a type of lending that is very speculative, and may only work in an increasing appreciation market. In other words, it may be good for a few years, but when the music stops and the market goes cold, I could see people losing whatever they had into a deal.

The marketing and advertisements also do not address the most bottom line result of a loan going bad and that is the foreclosure process. In general, that process is going to take six to twelve months depending on the area, which would be after the loan defaults, which in most states takes ninety to 120 days, plus legal fees to actually accomplish the task of foreclosing—all of which is not really covered or mentioned on any of the websites I have been reviewing. The way they split up the investment allows the money to be split among a larger number of investors, but may only be on one property. I could see this leading to issues for the smaller minor investors if a deal goes bad.

I think from the mortgage broker's perspective, you need to be aware of the things going on out there, but I really do not see how this type of lending is going to be successful long term. Eventually it will come under some type of regulation, because for all purposes it still involves lending money. I also do not think this is a safe vehicle for the new real estate investor, and as a mortgage professional, you should advise your clients as such. Real estate is not for everyone, but with lending standards loosening, people should focus on looking at traditional investor financing. There are several lenders that are now going back to ten total-financed properties, which is good, because some investors may have been stuck with the Fannie Mae rule of four total-financed properties. I would be ready to discuss something like this as just another potential investment idea, but it's not necessarily the same as owning the property yourself. If you think about it, if the total number is, say $100,000, and the minimum investment is $5,000, that would mean you could have potentially as many as twenty partners. That, in the long run, could be a major issue if the worst case scenario of foreclosure actually happens.

Be ready to discuss this type of item as a part of the overall real estate environment, but also keep in mind this would be something that could mean people are not actually acquiring financing from you. Be ready to point out the flaws in this type of investing versus an individual just obtaining the loan and owning the property themselves. Really, the answer is simple. You have a greater number of people splitting the risk, but the risk is the same—especially if they are looking at investing in a single property. If you are going to invest in a single property, you are better off owning it yourself than you are owning it with a large group of people. With this type of funding, the crowd is the issue. I belong in the category of people who would advise against this type of investment. This just sounds like it has too many opportunities that could expose investors to too much risk.

14

Useful Mortgage Websites

THE INTERNET IS full of useful sites for mortgage professionals. Here are some where you can sign up for daily newsletters, or just hop on to whenever you need to look for items.

www.ScotsmanGuide.com

One of the best overall resources for mortgage brokers and bankers. The Scotsman's Guide, if you are not already receiving it, will most likely eventually find its way to your doorstep. The online version has all the same features with a little less advertising. You can find information about investors, including products, states covered, and other opportunities. The magazine itself comes out once a month, and has two versions: one for residential and one for commercial.

www.BankersWeb.com

This is a newer site, and they specialize in webinars on various topics for financial users. I see a range of topics, including things like TRID, compliance, training modules, marketing, legal, and so on. These are not free webinars, but they are of value to you because you can improve your knowledge. They do offer a headlines section that covers relevant news and notes. Some topics you will see on there include updates on Dodd Frank and Cypersecurity.

www.MortgageNewsDaily.com

I like the format of this site. It also shows you a comparison of interest rates across the country, which is good to peek at each day if you are pricing your own loans to make sure you are staying competitive. There is also a leading indicator for bonds, etc. listed on this site. They offer webinars and other training courses, and appear to be set up in more of a question-and-answer format. They also have more technical numbers on this site, along with data on interest rates and where they are heading, or have been in the past. Overall a very good site if you are acting as your own secondary market maker.

15

Coaching/Mentoring

G IVEN THE AMOUNT of regulation and changes that constantly keep coming up in our industry, I think that investing in a coaching or mentoring program for oneself is a smart and prudent idea. There are a number of systems and services across the US that you can check out, and I want to go over a few of them. Mentoring is not for everyone due to the fact that most of these are web based, with contact mostly via phone. Some will offer services that can come to you, and some will offer training on-site for a cost. Cost for services will vary from coach to coach, and some of these are more along the lines of third-party support instead of hiring personnel. All of them can be resources for you to grow your business.

For a broker looking to open his own shop, I would suggest checking out the various levels of service, and I'll mention a few specifically by name that can be reached via their websites. This will be a level of service above a do-it-yourself, or self-paced, learning course. This is not for people beginning in the industry, per se; this is more for someone looking to take their brand or their branch to the next level with management or industry-specific training. I also want to highlight that a few of these guys are more along the lines of third-party compliance—I've lumped these in with the coaching/mentoring section because they can do more of a systems check for what you are doing, and could potentially keep you out of hot water with regulators. An ounce of prevention is worth a pound of the cure, and that is especially true in the mortgage industry. These are some examples of individuals offering services that can benefit you in setting up your business, training your people, and will help you take things to the next level.

From a coaching perspective, we have a few names to consider:

Deryck Cheyck is a sales trainer with more related to selling more mortgages. You can contact him at www. deryckcheney.com. His website offers free training videos, and you can register for further services to help grow your business. Deryck's site is very much geared toward applying a sales approach to mortgage training. He had a high-water mark of $110 million in loan volume in 2010. You can register on his website, and obtain some free initial training items.

Doug Thorpe is a mentor and trainer who has a background in mortgages, and he specializes in management training. You can find out more by visiting his website at: www.dougthorpe.com. He also has a newsletter that you can follow with further content regarding management information. His goal is to help first-time managers find health, wealth, and happiness while mastering the demands of teaching others. Doug spent his early years as a banker, and he uses the knowledge and experience he acquired from building other companies to teach managers to use their own leadership experience and skills. His teaching and techniques can be especially useful if you are relying on new managers to fill key roles or higher-up positions in your company.

Bill Kidwell provides information services to help you stay in front of changing regulations. His website can found at www.immaag.com. Bill formed a group with other like-minded mortgage professionals who came up with this simple message: the broker model offers consumers the best alternatives in lending. Bill has since furthered his brand and now offers training for newer loan officers. There is also a legislative advocacy component to the services Bill offers that is also found in the work he does helping support better regulations for our industry. He offers a subscription model with various services that align with the needs of a small brokerage owner.

Neill Fendly offers compliance and third-party auditing, and can be found at www.mortgage-defense.com . His company specializes in working with individuals from a preventative standpoint in regard to regulatory matters. I have personally worked with Neill, and found his expertise to be invaluable. He has helped my company with everything from employee issues to stress tests for our licensing practices across multiple states. Neill is a past president of NAMB, and has testified on behalf of the FBI in mortgage fraud cases. He has also received the United States Congressional Medal of Distinction. Neill is like an insurance policy for your mortgage business, and I would suggest anyone facing any type of regulatory action to give him a call. Also keep in mind, his services can help you avoid issues altogether by establishing strong policies and procedures from day one.

H.R. 2121 SAFE
Transitional Licensing Act 2015

As an update we have had a very positive move by our Federal Government in reference to the licensing for brokers. The SAFE transitional licensing act allows for brokers to have a provisional approval to move from banks or other states to give them a window to continue to work while their licensing is put into place either in a new state or more importantly a new employer

Anyone that has transitioned between two mortgages companies since the passing of the SAFE Act knows the frustration of not being active to conduct business. This has been a very limiting issue for any loan originator wanting to either change companies, relocate, or go from a bank to a brokerage.

With the passing of this provision in the SAFE ACT loan originators will now have more freedom to move between companies and states as they will have a 120-day window to work while their new licensing transitions. This will apply to movement between two companies as well as if you relocated across country from say Colorado to South Carolina. As long as you have a license in good standing or you work for a bank as an active originator then you can transition under this new law.

This makes the last section of my book even more relevant as Bankers will now be able to move to independent brokers more easily.

SECTION 3:

How to Convert
to a Broker After
Being a Banker

16

Banker to Broker

IN GENERAL, MORTGAGE professionals have faced a lot of challenges in the last few years. From the elimination of yield-spread premium to the creation of the NMLS system, we have faced numerous hurdles, and not all of us made it through these difficult times. Let's face it: the days of the rogue loan officer making five points on credit-challenged borrowers are relegated to the past, and removing those individuals from the industry is the best for everyone. The guys that are just out to make a fast buck are going to be selling cars, calling themselves developers, or pursuing some other shady, get-rich-quick type of business; however, you can guarantee what they won't be doing, which is legally selling loans. With the "culling of the herd," so to speak, we now have accepted industry standards that we can all follow—and thrive under—if these are adhered to properly. There's plenty of money on the table to be made; it's just a matter of knowing your craft, and knowing how to get set up so you're able to access the money that *is* out there.

In my opinion, we're going to see growth when it comes to individuals transitioning from bankers to brokerage who want to migrate to better wage scales. I think we will see two kinds of brokers: the one-man shop, and the small shop that's built around one high-volume loan officer. My group would be the latter, where I have assembled a senior processing staff, and I have several junior loan officers who work my lead systems and bring in the applications. We operate much like a doctor's office, where each deal is brought to my desk and reviewed, priced, and, in turn, sold and processed. I think that my model is going to be very successful, and this model is what people who are starting out as one-man shops will seek to grow in to as the industry stabilizes. Our last section is geared toward bankers, and will address those who are looking for better compensation that can be obtained by transitioning to a career as a mortgage broker. The terms are all loosely fitting; however, they basically all surround the same concept, which is you owning and operating your own shop. In this last section, I will also address resource materials and best practices. I will admit, we broke a lot of eggs along the way, but hopefully this section will help people who have decided to to make this transition.

Banks around the country took the opportunity afforded them by Dodd Frank to drastically constrict and change compensation for their loan officers. Most banks are now paying their loan officers anywhere from fifty-five to a hundred basis points, tops, and are drastically cutting down on any fees paid to refinance their clients. That said, the real pressure is on the traditional bank loan officer to always bring in new business.

Banks do have some unique product offerings, but let's take a deeper look at the overall comparison between mortgage broker and banker. For the purposes of this discussion, I'll refer to anyone who works at a traditional bank, such as Wells Fargo, Bank of America, Suntrust, or any other big-box bank, as a banker. I do not make this comparison in regard to correspondent lenders, who could also be considered bankers. In general, a banker is anyone who is lending their company's own money at the closing table. We'll now touch on some of the differences between a broker and a banker, and we'll then go into a detailed plan of attack for anyone who no longer wants to continue being underpaid as a banker, and who wants to open their own small-to-medium sized mortgage broker company. I will also go into detail regarding the difference between being a broker and a banker, and the necessary steps to achieve both types of lending under your own name.

The simplest way to put it is this: As a broker or a correspondent, you will make more money than you will as a banker. Banks like to sell a popular myth regarding their stability and the claim they're able to create business for you as a loan officer. The reality is that, while the label on the door is important, the person behind the label is ultimately the most important reason a person uses your services. There are cases to be made for a unique product that's being offering by a bank, but do those benefits outweigh the additional compensation you can receive on a daily basis when you own your own shop? Speaking as someone who has been on both sides of the fence (although I was only briefly working at a bank and it was over ten years ago), the further restrictions most banks place on their loan officers when it comes to compensation combined with volume limits, along with their stance on your past clients, working at a bank could likely end up being a futile enterprise for any officer who does less than $ 3-4 million a month. That's not to say that a bank loan officer who closes in excess of $3 million has it made. They are, in most cases, vastly underpaid, but anyone who makes less than those volume numbers is going to have a hard time reaching success levels I feel are a requirement for my loan officers.

Let's look at just the basics in terms of the compensation model. Let's compare a bank loan officer making sixty-five basis points and a fairly standard broker model of one hundred basis points. The math here is very simple: the broker is making 35 percent more than the banker.

So for every one million in production, the bank loan officer makes $6,500 for the month, while the broker makes $10,000. That's of course pre-taxes, and the numbers go out from there. Compare the two for a year, and you have a salary of $78,000, while the other ends up making $120,000—when they've both done the same amount of volume. That's a very big difference, especially if you are creating your business and leads.

The only real exception I've found to this is is when your primary line of business involves a niche product not offered by any brokerage channels. A few examples of this would be larger construction deals, or a 100 percent doctor's loan. There are options to do construction lending as a broker, but before you jump on that boat, please know they're facing a unique set of challenges with TRID regarding how they disclose to borrowers. Flagstar is rumored to be rolling out a doctor's loan in 2016.

Now consider some of the restrictions faced by bankers. I am seeing more and more banks consider past clients to be their clients, and paying a far lower commission rate—sometimes as low as twenty-five basis points for refinance transactions. I also am seeing, on average, that banks have a cut off of 640 when it comes to credit scores, rates that tend to be twenty-five basis points higher, with very few niche products on offer. For most of your larger banks, the flexibility is simply not there, and you can look no further than 2008 to understand why. All the banks we're talking about here have made a decision to no longer be in the wholesale arena on a daily basis, and instead they've raised their standards to where they now only primarily work as a paper business from their retail store fronts. The reason is obvious: the *risk* associated with the home loan, as well as the *cost* it requires to offer services to their clients. Almost any banker would tell you they have much higher costs due to the brick and mortar, the overhead required to be a bank, as well as the regulations involved. What we have seen since the meltdown, is that all the big banks are pulling out of wholesale, and placing themselves in much larger- scale relationships with fewer key lenders. They no longer offer wholesale models to the "mom and pop" mortgage broker, and instead do business with the larger, mid-level players and charge them a premium for any loans they do from their retail branches. They changed their model, which does not necessarily mean they changed it for the betterment of their own loan officers. If the bank is not creating business for you, then you need to strongly consider all your options, namely becoming a broker.

This brings me to the point I want to emphasize in this last section of the book. As the housing market becomes stable, we'll see a return migration from the banker model to the broker model. There will be changes and hurdles to overcome, which I hope to explain here, that will help bankers who've made the decision to open their own shop by offering a field guide on all there is to know about making this important transition. In my opinion, if you can self-generate over $2 million in loan volume per month on average, you will be better off, and your efforts will be more profitable as a mortgage broker than they would be as a banker. This is not to say that if you depend on the bank to generate your leads, you couldn't possibly achieve success, but if you are ultimately the reason the phone rings, and you do the aforementioned volume, then you are losing money every day you work for a bank. The steps required to open your own shop aren't as difficult as they seem, and I hope that this book can help you make the transition.

With any employment transition you need to make sure you have covered as many of your bases in advance as possible. For our purposes here, I'll assume you are making a plan in advance of your departure from your current employer, and that you are opening your own shop. If you are simply going from a bank to a correspondent, or to work for a broker, then this isn't necessarily geared toward your situation. That would be a simpler change of employment, and for that what really only matters is how your licensing is handled, which does not involve many of the following steps I am about to discuss in detail.

Starting your own mortgage brokerage shop presents its own unique set of challenges, and with the recent advent of the NMLS, it has become a little harder, most notably due to the fact that you can't work at two mortgage companies at one time. What this means in the real world is that a banker leaving his or her bank will have some down time between their migration from banker to owning their own company. Most states also require at least two years in banking or mortgage brokerage as a licensed loan officer prior to establishing your own shop.

With this in mind, timing is everything when you make your plan, and I want to lay out a few items you can do in advance to get yourself ready. First and foremost, you can set up your LLC and company name, and get your paperwork in line with the state. You will need the active tax identification number to complete the next steps. Once you have your company named, and your tax ID in place, you can apply with NMLS to get your company number; however, you will not be able to get an approved license yet.

The time of year is also a key factor due to that fact that all states have now moved to December 31 as the end of the calendar year. If you apply for your license at the end of the year, say in October, you would have to renew and pay duplicate fees for the following year. I would recommend that anyone starting out should begin preparation in late summer to early fall with setting up your LLC, making sure you have your arrangements for continuing education in line, any website development, and branding all done prior to applying for NMLS licensure status. The new LLC, or My Mortgage Company, LLC, will have to get its own unique NMLS license number. You can obtain this number without triggering a change to your personal NMLS number, and you can get this number before applying for any new licenses in a state. All states' licensing for new applications and renewal open on December 1, so at that point you can apply for the licensing for your new entity. Be prepared, however, that at this point you will have to have a member of the LLC who has an active NMLS number ready to be listed as the qualified individual. Someone has to be attached to the new NMLS number for My Mortgage Company, LLC, because your current-future-past employer will be notified that this individual has removed their license from their company, and is now with My Mortgage Company, LLC. In other words, that person has now reached the point of no return, will no longer be able to originate at their current employer, and will be forced to wait until the new company is active and approved with investors.

As part of your set up, you should be speaking with investors about your new venture, but you will obviously want to keep this talk to a minimum, as you are still working for someone else. My recommendation is to initially get set up with no more than one or two key investors, just so you're able to keep things simple and quiet. The investors themselves will not be able to approve you until you have both the approved entity (My Mortgage Company) and an approved, qualified individual for that entity. Once you have approval from your home state for both the entity and the qualified individual, then you can get approval with your investor. Expect for this process to take up most of December by the time you've obtained approvals by the state, and then by the investors a few weeks after that. In a perfect world, you will be ready to go by mid-January, or in about forty-five days. From a licensing standpoint, December is the ideal month to begin so you don't have to pay the fees twice; however, this is also a traditionally slower time of year. During the holidays, there are less people who buying homes, so you are missing the business that would ordinarily allow you to quickly get your venture up and running. Also keep in mind, you can't really market until you have your unique identifiers and licensing in order.

Office space is also an important factor to consider. All licensing will require a physical location for you to practice mortgage licensing. Speaking from experience, I recommend starting off small. Consider your short-term options when it comes to office space, which includes executive offices. An office can provide a professional work space at a fraction of the cost with no long-term commitment. When you think logically about the turnaround time it takes to close a loan, the industry has about a twenty-five- to thirty-day cycle for you to receive cash flows. We are not an industry where the receivables come in quickly, and if you use a warehouse line selling loans off your line.

You will see a further delay when it comes to warehouse lending, and the cash flows can potentially take ten to fiftenn days on top of the normal closing schedule. That said, from day one as you begin to plan, keep in mind the amount of your projected cash flows, and how that could affect you month to month. Office space for our industry is a necessity, but your location may not be that important depending on how you plan to market. If you're planning to work the Internet, become involved in new home communities, and network among realty shops, you will be spending a decent amount of time out of the office, so this is definitely something to consider. You need to have a space that's practical, but also affordable. I recommend erring on the side of caution, which means focusing your money on your marketing, and your message to your consumers, especially when you're just getting started. You want the consumer and your referral partners to buy in to your abilities and to be convinced of what you can offer, so be sure to focus on delivering good products and services, and not the expensive overhead.

I've compiled a list of necessary requirements/issues you'll need to address before you're able to get your company on board with licensing and investor approvals:

- Plan for your office space.
- Choose your operating software.

- Set up your credit vendor.
- Order business cards, and include your NMLS number in your business card design.
- Acquire client management software if this is not already part of your operating system.
- Come up with a marketing plan and schedule.
- Prep for any leads you plan to order.
- Have a compliance plan.
- If you have employees, have contracts ready.
- Cover any needs under Obamacare.
- Obtain any necessary business licenses from local regulatory bodies (city).
- Order office supplies, but be sure to look for discounts.
- Weigh out your processing options.

These are mistakes to avoid when you first start out:

- Do not make costly commitments for phone services or phone contracts; look at Internet phones instead.
- Do not buy expensive copiers or Internet service.
- Do not try to obtain bonding and licensing in too many states at one time; these costs can get out of hand.
- Watch your healthcare costs.
- Avoid pricy furniture—it's just a desk; it's not that special.
- Avoid overstaffing.

Now that we have our planning and preparation done, it is time to make the move. The first step is to properly close out, and end your existing relationship. In my experience, for you to be able to get paid from old business, the status of said business must either be clear or in its closing stages. You also want to keep in mind that contractually you are most likely required to leave any past clients behind.

In reality, most loan officers keep a separate database of any past clients and referral partners.

Once your transition is in process, and you've acquired your licensing. The first, and most important, step is to get the word out regarding your change in career, which you can start by changing your information on any social media platforms, such as Linkedin and Facebook. I would also write a personal, handwritten card to send to your top referral partners, in addition to a post card announcement that will go out to past clients with your new current contact information. I also recommend you include information on any new products and services you're offering as a broker, and highlight the key differences with each.

A few key points to make to your past clients regarding your services:

- You offer lower rates and unique products.
- You can potentially lower credit scores.
- You also offer niche products for self-employed individuals.

- Let them know you will contact them each year for annual reviews.

The real key when it comes to your initial contact—whether it be electronic, through the mail, or both— is to get your new brand name and contact information out to these people as soon as possible, because you'll want to start building brand awareness for your new firm. Remember you are building a brand, so as many meetings and opportunities you have to get the word out will benefit you going forward.

Word of mouth and social media will help get you started, but you'll also need a solid lead source—most likely Internet leads—to supplement your new company as you get going. This is important, as you will need to have planned ahead on the licenses you need to market across multiple states. Remember, you can't market or quote rates in states where you are not licensed, so this needs to have been covered during your set-up process. As your licenses become approved, you can begin to purchase leads. The lead company themselves won't do much—if any— research to see if you are licensed, because, as the owner of the company, this is your responsibility.

As the owner of your company, let's go over some topics from an operations standpoint with which you'll need to become familiar:

Investors are the partners for both a broker and lender who will lend your clients money, and getting them on board should be one of your first steps. Franklin American and Flagstar Wholesale are two investors that I have found to be user friendly when it comes to setting up your business.

Commergence is a new company that acts as a clearing house for your investors to be able to get approvals done for your firm. They will handle any documents you upload for your investors, store them on their server, and will then e-mail you a document request from your investors. So, for example, if you work with a lender who wants quarterly financials, you will receive an e-mail asking you to upload these requested documents. Most of your "heavy lifting" when it comes to using this system is based upon your renewal periods with your lenders, but should plan to be done at the first of the year.

Quickbooks is a must have for any new mortgage broker business owner. All investors are going to require financials on your company as you get started, and to continue your relationship with them. You need to be on top of your books, and be ready to finish them each month. Most investors, if they want something from you, will be looking for quarterly reports and year-end statements. If you are doing warehouse lending, then you will have asset requirements where you may need to submit a detailed profit-loss-and-balance sheet at any given time.

Insurance requirements will differ per state, but you will need to have surety bonds in place, as well as Errors and Omissions Insurance. You will also need a fidelity bond if you have employees. If you offer health insurance, you will need to have a uniform policy for your employees— whether that means they must pay 50 percent of the premium, or they won't be offered health insurance at all. Make sure you are in compliance with Obamacare.

Compliance, policies, and procedures need to be in written format via employee handbooks, which you'll also distribute then to your investors. All of your investors will want to have written steps regarding your company's methods for handling your loans. You'll find examples of employee handbooks, policies and procedures, disaster plans, etc. in the appendix of this book. You'll need to tailor these templates to fit your company's needs. but they can act as a road map to help guide you in the right direction.

Appraisal management companies is another aspect where you will have to make decisions as a mini-correspondent lender. You are the lender of your own money, so you will get to select a management company, and then set the appraisers on your list. You'll still have to deal with all the legalities involved, which means you won't be allowed to contact them during the process, or influence their decisions, but you do have the advantage of getting to choose who you want to work with as a team. You will set a standard rotation for the realtors on your list, and they will bid out for the appraisals your company does on the warehouse line. This does not mean you can call them, but it does mean you can set up a team of professionals who understand your market. Also, by having the AMC, this gives you access to other realtors in markets in other parts of the state or country. If you find yourself doing business in another area of your home state, if you've found people who do quality work, you can set up these appraisers to cover these other territories. Everything is held and managed in compliance with all local, state, and federal laws, but, again, you have the advantage of knowing you'll work with in advance.

Credit vendors are an essential part of any mortgage broker's business and lender's world. You need their product to make your credit decisions, and run your approvals on your operating software. Two key items to consider when choosing a vendor, are the cost and amount of services they offer. In the last few years, the number of items passed back to the lender (you) to cover part of your credit package has increased. In the past you could simply pull a fifteen- to twenty-five-dollar report, and that was the end of it. Now your investors pass a number of expenses back to you via your credit services, namely credit supplements, reissuing the reports, and the number of runs they do during the underwriting process. We have seen the cost go all the way up to eighty to a hundred dollars per client when acting as a lender. You do not see these same charges passed back as a broker. This is important, because if you do not disclose the correct fee, you will not be able to collect it on the settlement statement. More importantly, an incorrect disclosure comes out of your pocket. Make sure, as the owner of the company, you are accurately estimating the true cost of the report before you disclose this to the client. It is also important to remember that some items cannot be charged to the client, such as work done for a re-score. Those are costs that you have to take on as a broker in order to make your deal work—you cannot make the client pay for a re-score. You can pass along the supplements, do additional pulls if necessary, and re-issuance costs on the settlement statement if you disclose these again prior to closing. All invoices for these costs have to be placed on the settlement statement, and given to closing agents and your investors.

The takeaway for the new brokerage owner transitioning from the world of banking is this: the costs involved with this change in career can get high for a small broker owner very, very quickly if these costs are not managed. We do a mid-month check on the credit account to see what charges need to be added and then disclosed again before closing. I have my closer double check the amounts prior to issuing documents as well.

I know of some brokerage firms that will charge a credit report fee up front—keep in mind, however, that you can only charge the exact amount of the invoice.

You credit vendors are aware of the issues for lenders, so they have created a few all-in-one credit-file products so you can better disclose these numbers to your clients. For example, our credit vendor, Credit Technologies, offers a fifty-five- dollar, one-time credit report fee that covers all your supplements, reissuance fees, and anything else short of a re-score. The one downside to this product is that if you pull lower scores that cause you to be disqualified, you'll still be charged the same cost unless you set up a feature that puts a one-score-only issue on the report for anyone with collections, for a score below 620, and for public records. You can set that feature for a one score only, and the cost drops down to seven dollars, which lets you know you have a credit-challenged borrower prior to pulling the other two bureaus in the file. It will basically give you a chance to look at the report to see if there are any deal killers prior to spending the money to get the rest of the scores. If you pull someone with lower scores, this can be very handy, and it can save you time and effort when you see a major issue in their file, such as large collections or judgments.

Third-party document preparation companies will also be part of your new life when you get to the mini-correspondent level, as they will be responsible or preparing your documents to send to the closing agents. They also handle your closing disclosures now, post-TRID. There are currently still some issues when you try to get your own software to prepare closing disclosures. There was a significant glitch in the system that caused escrow aggregation, and to prepare these requires specific software that would be cost prohibitive for a small mortgage shop. This makes a third-party document preparation company a necessary part of the equation, even though this service means an added expense for the consumer.

17

Employees

As you grow your business, you will need to rely on others for their assistance in the production aspects of the business. I find that in order to have a significant volume of business, you'll need processing support, junior loan officers, and assistants. When you start out, these are a few key things to keep in mind when you hire your first employees:

- Make sure you have employee contracts and handbooks in place.
- All loan officers are required to have a contract in compliance with Dodd Frank.
- Your processing staff need to have written policies and procedures.

- Make sure you have state and federal employment rules posted somewhere on-site.
- Make sure you have a business license if one is required by your city or county.
- Your loan officer licenses should be displayed. (This is not a rule in every state.)

Another thing to remember, is that each loan officer has to have a specific compensation plan in order to be compliant with Dodd Frank. For example, my contracts have two forms of compensation to the loan officer. I typically pay fifty to seventy-five basis points, depending on experience, for deals that I've generated through my marketing efforts. I will then pay the same loan officer 125 basis points for deals they've self-generated, and brought in via their own marketing efforts. This is an example of a compliant-compensation model. The compensation amount must be consistent, and should not give any incentive for the loan officer to charge a higher rate in order to increase his or her own personal compensation. Keep in mind that this is an employee's payment, and based upon the broker (or warehouse) model, you will have more money to work with as your profit.

It is also fairly standard to charge a processing fee as well, but depending on your investors you may not be able to charge one unless you are acting as a mini-correspondent, which means you can act as your own secondary market and do your own pricing. You will still have to pay your loan officer based upon their compensation plan, however. For that very reason I make sure I am the only one who does my pricing, and the only one who locks the loans on the warehouse line. I typically shoot for a minimum of three hundred basis points, with a processing fee and bonus built in to that number, which makes this model far more profitable.

A word to the wise, from a flow standpoint, I keep the processors separate from the sales floor. It is very difficult to hone in on the numerous items you must deal with to get loans done if there are sales people hovering around who are also trying to get their deals done. Personally, I keep myself on the processing side of things so I can manage what's going on, and to keep my sales people out of the processors' hair. My system lets the salespeople turn over the files so others can then assist them, because they need to be on the phones worknig to get more deals—not ordering payoffs or tracking down homeowner's insurance. It is very important to structure, and clearly define, each person's role in the process of creating our production.

18

Warehouse-Line Lending

ONCE YOU HAVE established a pipeline with your first investors, you will need to focus not only on closing your loans, but you expanding your product offerings. As part of your marketing plan, you will need to have identified the investors you want to work with, and then have taken the steps to get approved with each of them. As a broker, this process is rather simple, but this also brings us the decision as to whether you want to become a mini-correspondent with some of your investors. Many brokers decide that they are just fine with the compensation structure they've set up with their investors under Dodd Frank, which would be anywhere from a hundred to three hundred basis points. Most veterans will decide that it's more profitable to become a mini-correspondent.

Being a mini-correspondent means that you do not actually underwrite your files, but you do act as the funder, or the seller, of your own paper. There are certain requirements you must have in place in order to become a mini-correspondent, so keep in mind this won't be for everyone. The investor will be doing the underwriting of your loan with an agreement to purchase this loan directly from you. You will have a limited amount of risk as a mini-correspondent since you are not, in fact, underwriting the file. The investor will also be working with you to sell the loan off the line.

Under this method, your compensation method of lending is known as a Service Release Premium, or SRP. Your premium is paid at the time of sale, which is typically five to ten business days after the funding of the loan. You will have to pay interest to carry on with your loans from your premium.

You first have to look at the levels of bonding and licensing you need for your particular state to become a mini-correspondent or mortgage lender. This terminology means the same things, which is that you have the ability to have a warehouse line and close loans in your own name. You will also need to have your financials in order, and be able to show a minimum net worth of typically fifty thousand dollars to open a line. There are a number of warehouse-line providers across the country, and finding one who you can work with is key in order for you to grow your business.

You may be questioning why you would want to go the trouble of becoming a warehouse-line lender? The answer is simple. You will receive better pricing for your loans, and you can have hold backs paid to you as a monthly bonus. Some lenders will pay these per loan, but it is pretty standard to get a hold back, or bonus check, once a month. A pretty standard hold back amount from pricing would be at least a hundred basis points. In the real world, I can have a hold back of a hundred basis points, and I would still be priced at one hundred basis points better than my competitors, especially when it comes to the banks in my area. This leads to more profitability if you handle your line correctly. Keep in mind that you are going to see an increase in the number of fees required. Let's detail the additional items you need to have covered in your fees. These include:

- Any documentation preparation fees from your third-party vendor
- A wire fee
- The interest-rate carry on your line
- The underwriting fee to your investor
- The annual audit fee, which amounts to roughly between $8,000 and $12,000 per year
- The increase in insurance coverage above broker
- Any third-party compliance charges

You can pass the majority of these fees on to the HUD, and still have superior pricing. The key is to make sure you are pricing loans accordingly on your line. I find that you need to average 250 basis points, plus a processing fee and your bonus. This will still keep you priced in front of your competitors, and keep your business profitable. Early on in my career as warehouse lender, we were priced too low on our hold back. We did have some of the best rates in the country, and as a matter of fact, we were noted in the Wall Street Journal for having the best rates in the country. The only problem was that for us to keep up with the regulations and compliance, we were priced *too low* on our loans. We were actually giving out rates that were too good to cover costs, an important balancing act. One of the most important aspects in making the decision to be a warehouse lender relates to your ability to control your pricing, while simultaneously balancing your overhead costs. I believe you can make substantially more money as a mini-correspondent if you price your loans properly. This is why I act as my own secondary in terms of pricing every loan for my team of loan officers who are under me. You can use loan pricing software, like Optimal Blue or Loansifter, to price your loans so you're able to get the best daily pricing; however, I've honestly found that to be too difficult on the back end for your processing staff, since we do not underwrite our own files. Instead, I have moved to a model where I am holding back a larger bonus to maintain our monthly overhead and expenses in our pricing, which allows you to not mistakenly price loans. It also creates a savings account of sorts that you can plan to use to regulate your cash flow. All of this can be done while maintaining your pricing advantage in comparison to the rest of the market. Your pricing advantage will be obvious, especially on government loans, like VA and USDA, both of which can be put on my warehouse line.

Currently, the FHA still requires a Full Eagle Licensing Approval, so right now I broker all of my FHA loans with a 250-basis-point compensation plan. A Full Eagle License has higher net-worth standards for the company, and increased levels of regulation that may make it too cumbersome for a smaller mortgage brokerage shop. Net worth aside, the increased costs for audits and other reporting translates to needing to produce higher volumes of FHA loans. If you are going to get your Full Eagle, you may as well higher an underwriter, and do your own loans in-house as a full correspondent. This is more of a risk reward, and not something you would start out doing in your first few years of owning your own shop.

I am a strong supporter of becoming a mini-correspondent lender as soon as possible. Net worth requirements, costs, and increased work are worth it to achieve a greater amount of profitability. You will most likely have to start out as a broker, but only as you build your company, and the net worth of the company. Once you are ready, I suggest you transition from this to a mini-correspondent or lender. I also recommend you maintain your ability to broker deals, because this is how you will be able to offer niche products, do FHA, and hard-money transactions. The licensing for these is different in some states, but once you go lender, you typically maintain the ability to be a broker. In some states, like Virginia, you can be both a lender and a broker, and they have different requirements in terms of bonding. There is nothing to stop you from choosing to be a lender in some states, and a broker in others. For example, I am a lender in South Carolina, but I am a broker only in Virginia; therefore, we only use brokerage services in the state of Virginia, and we cannot use our warehouse line in that state. This is a strategic move, because I focus my marketing efforts on my purchase business in my home state, and if we do mailers in other states they are primarily for FHA or VA—both of which can easily be brokered with my investors. The flexibility of being able to lend to match your marketing plan is a distinct advantage for a mortgage broker. The pricing advantage of the warehouse line does make it possible for you to be a lender in each state, as long as you are getting the type of business to make it worth your time and to justify the added expense.

Being a warehouse lender, you do need to have a clear marketing plan to make the extra expense worthwhile. Currently, it makes the most sense for us—as a shop that does primarily a 50/50 split of purchase to refinance—I put all our purchase business and loans over $200,000 on to our warehouse line. All loans under $200,000, and FHA loans, are put through broker channels. I am seeing roughly a 50/50 mix between what we put on the line and what we are brokering. You will be very tempted to put every loan on the line when you are getting started, but let me give you a few pointers as to why this is not a great idea in the current market.

First, from a cash flow standpoint you need to remember that a refinance will typically have a four-day right of rescission that you have to account for prior to the actual funding of a loan. For the warehouse line, this means that you can't do much to get the loan sold, because it hasn't technically been funded. Depending on your closing attorney, they may also have not returned the note, which is really when your work to sell your loan can begin. You can communicate with the closing attorney, and ask them to return the note, but nothing is guaranteed until the point of funding. Most attorneys will want to hold the note just in case the client changes their mind. Well, that means you can add one more day to the funding date, and then you will have five business days added to funding a refinance transaction.

Purchases on your line will be overnighted, and back to your investor the next day in most cases. With refinances, just by the nature of their function, automatically give you five more business days, or one full week, longer to do your funding on this type of loan. Investment property refinances would fund similar to purchases. The normal refinances will take longer to get off your line, and this will add to delays as to when you get the funds into your bank. These delays are on top of the delays that occurred prior to closing with TRID. TRID is currently taking, on average, forty-eight hours to get out a closing disclosure via the third-party documentation preparation, and then a three-day hold prior to going to a closing—which puts another four days in front of your closing, stretching out the days between paychecks even further.

A second factor to keep in mind is the additional cost required to close a warehouse loan. There is a trade off in being able to make more on those loans via the SRP you receive when you sell it, but there are additional costs passed through to your borrowers. The smaller the loan, the higher these fees look in comparison to the same deal you could offer to your client as a broker. On average, I have found the additional cost to be about a thousand dollars once you factor in the warehouse-line usage and third-party documentation preparation fees. The lower rate we can offer on the warehouse line is not worth the additional costs on the smaller-sized loans.

My strategy is to keep the smaller loans moving through the system faster, which will allow you to get the money in the bank. The larger loans, where you can really take advantage of your pricing structure, should be put on the warehouse line, especially your purchases. Cash flow is king, and you have to have loans coming in to create your pipeline, but you also have to be able to convert those loans in to money. Keep the money moving, and keep them closing.

19

Work Flow

GETTING STARTED AS a broker won't be that different from your work flow as a banker. You may have more upfront you have to work on (in terms of a learning curve) when it comes to the documents and figuring out procedures, but the playing field is pretty level now with TRID, and your investors should do a good job keeping you informed of when things need to go out and whether things are correct.

Most of you will not be starting out as a lender or mini-correspondent, so you will be relying on your investors for some of your disclosures, especially at the end of the process after you receive your clear to close. Before we discuss those items, however, let's look at an average work flow for a one-man shop just getting started out in the industry.

The first step is to take a perfect application for your borrower. From there, everything else should flow in a uniform direction. As long as the coordinates on the map are put in correctly, it should make getting the ship to port no problem. If you make errors in your application, you will have errors in your process to get the loan closed. The document preparation portion of the application will come from both your operating system and the investor who will be sending a copy over as well.

I will point out that often times what the investor sends over does not coincide 100 percent with what your actual numbers are, so you may want to prepare your consumer. The reason I say this is that sometimes the investor's forms can be more confusing, because they usually just put out a blanket e-mail once you register a loan. If the hard copy file has not been uploaded to their system to show the actual fees, there could be some overestimation on their part. This can be confusing to the consumer, and will be a problem, especially for a first-time home buyer because they may not understand the differences. I would suggest making the consumer aware of this prior to when it could potentially cause issues for you.

Once the documents have gone out to your consumer and have come back in, it is time to put your files together. Some bankers may not be used to the actual process of putting together a file depending on how this was previously structured, so I've included a checklist we use for our file conversions that gives you a piece-by-piece order of steps for putting together files to submitted for underwriting. This can be found in our appendix, and I would suggest you e-mail me if you would like a PDF version you can use if you don't want to put one together on your own.

A simple checklist, it will let you make sure you are matching up items from your approval that you have run on your operating system. We also take the extra step of printing up our files so we can have a hard copy with contact information placed on the outside cover that includes the name of the lender, the closing attorney, the insurance agent, realtors, lock timeline, and, most importantly, the closing date. Once we finish with a file, we upload these items into our storage software, and then safely shred the file.

You need to get in the habit of making sure you collect your closing documents from your closing attorney, including a fully signed HUD, a breakdown of the fees, and a copy of the note. All of these will come in handy later, and all of them will be documents you have to collect to move into mini-correspondent, so you may as well start collecting them from day one, even as a broker.

When it comes to selling your loans off your warehouse line, you need to start to be ready for post-closing, and the requirements it will take to actually sell your loan. Typically, with your mini-correspondent lenders, you will have to comply with all final closing documents to sell the loan and receive your payment, or the service release premium. The SRP is your paycheck, and keep in mind that the SRP is going to be derived from your lock, minus all the carrying costs of the loan, including the interest, wire fees, and any other bank fees. You will be able to pass along some of the bank fees to the client via the wire fee, but the interest carry will be something that is charged to you. This means the faster you get the loans sold off your line equals to more money saved for you.

As a mini-correspondent, you will have assistance from the documentation preparation company and some help from the investor, but I recommend once you reach this level, that you have your closer handle this, or that you handle it yourself. Nobody is going to be more responsible for getting your loan sold than the person who receives the paycheck. A good closer is really a requirement of obtaining this level of lending, because it would be next to impossible for the owner of the company to wear all these hats.

I choose to focus my efforts on the sale aspect of our business—I get the loans in the door, and I have a support staff that works the loans in a method similar to an assembly line. I have one person for making sure the documents go out, locks get input after my approval, and when paperwork comes back from the borrower, I also have my junior loan officers work on all document collection from their clients when they have meetings in person. Once we have a file put together, the next step follows, and the file is given to my second-level processor for submission to clear to close. Finally, the loan goes to the my closer, and she handles the preparation of all our documents. For brokered loans, we just have the first two processors handle the file, and then my closer approves the final HUD and collects our post-closing items.

Everything working in connection with the other lets us effectively move loans across multiple lenders with a high volume amount of business coming in. The same process can be achieved by a single correspondent, because they will underwrite the file based upon different standards to sell them post-closing. This is a difference between mini -correspondent and correspondent. My method does require more overhead in terms of people, but at the same time it allows for compartmentalization of your process. Each brokerage can set up their structure as they see fit, which is the best structure for how we are currently doing business. A smaller operation could accomplish similar results, but I would recommend drastically cutting back on your lenders, and to potentially only use no more than one or two. The flexibility this system allows for is key to being able to offer multiple pricing levels, and multiple lenders products. It is what works best for us, which is the most important thing to figure out for any brokerage firm—what works. Become an expert at perfecting your work flow system so that you're able to maintain a high level of customer service and close your loans on time, all while being profitable.

20

Compliance

I think one of the areas where there may be similarities between being a banker and a broker is in the compliance department. Bankers should be fairly used to having to deal with regulation via the bank, and it's pretty much the same for brokers, only you'll be doing a large portion of it yourself.

I'll now discuss s few key items that any banker opening his own branch needs to be aware of as he gets started. You want to break down your compliance in two parts: NMLS and licensing, and state regulation. I pretty much covered the NMLS portion of this earlier, but, going forward, you'll need to comply with your continuing education and make sure you are taking all the bonding and renewal steps per state you must do as a broker.

A second layer of the compliance onion relates to call reports, third-party compliance, and any quality control reviews you do for your company. Let's start with a call report. I am going to attach a copy of one of these in the appendix. A call report, per state, will be due quarterly, and will be generated from the loans in your operating system. The format for each state's call report is a little different in what they require you to submit, but they are all basically the same. It is a record of the loans that you closed in that quarter, as well as a list of the loans denied or in process. Be aware that failure to turn in call reports on time will result in fines, and an incomplete call report could potentially lead to audits (a topic we'll cover later in this chapter).

Some states also require that you be able to generate the reports from your software, and this could require software upgrades that can cost you additional money, so be prepared for increasing costs in order to remain in compliance.

A secondary type of report that some states may request is a quality control report, or a QC report. What this basically means is that you, or someone who works for you, has performed some type of inspection of closed loans. This is more realistic if you have loan officers working under you. In my case, I come in contact with each loan prior to even submitting it, so it does add a layer of protection at the front gate. The larger you get, the more it becomes a necessary step in the process that someone spot checks and audits your files, much like if the state were to come in. A third-party company, like Mortgage Defense (www.mortgage-defense.com), can come into your firm, and they will audit 10 percent more of your files versus what's looked at with a state regulatory checklist. Again, the larger you get, the more necessary this step becomes. Be prepared for this to cost you several thousand dollars, but, comparatively speaking, getting fined or getting in trouble with the state could cause you to potentially lose your license.

I suggest another service they offer, which is more along the lines of a self-evaluation, or a stress-test. You can perform this to see if your practices are compliant, and whether your people are following them. If you set a standard, you need to confirm they are following your guidelines, or you are the one left exposed at the end of the day. Remember, they fine the owner of the company, not the employee who made the mistake.

One question I get from a lot of people starting out is where to get these types of items to train their employees. The answer is actually pretty simple: You can look online at some of the training centers, like www.training-pro.com, but you can also rely on your investors. Most of them will have educational webinars and training you can arrange on your own for yourself and your processors. A few big ones that have been popular here recently include

Anti Money Laundering, TRID training, and compliance items in general per investor. The best part about the training tools with these investors is that they are *free*. As you are getting started out on your own, I would recommend spending at least an hour a week reviewing or taking a webinar so you can keep in touch with compliance-related items.

With compliance, you could go on and on for a long time trying to figure out what is what, but the key is that you know where to find an answer when a question comes up. This kind of goes back to one of the first pieces of advice I laid out, which is to keep your lending options simple when you're starting out. That way you can have just a few key points of contact to make sure you are doing things the right way.

Overall, in order to remain compliant, follow the Golden Rule: Do unto others as you would have them do unto you. Always look at it from your customer's perspective to see whether it looks and sounds right and is what you would expect if you were in their shoes. I would caution you that states are looking for missing items, and not just making sure things were done properly—but for any potential items missing that could open you up to fines and or audits. Remember, all states now allow you to store your files in your software online or in a cloud. You do not need the paper files lying around—if anything, that is more dangerous.

21

Audits

A STATE-DONE AUDIT can seem like a very challenging prospect, but if you have been doing things the right way, and keeping up with proper documentation and storage of these documents, you will have a leg up in preparation for an audit by a state regulator.

A few things to keep in mind when preparing for an audit: First, an audit is typically announced well in advance, so this will give you time to tidy up any housekeeping items in preparation for it. The auditor is going to be there on behalf of the state, and depending on the guidelines for your state, they could be there on your dime. It is not uncommon for you to have to pay for them to audit you—that's right—you have to compensate the state for them to do an audit of your files. The reality is that if you have everything in place, then the audit should go smoothly and you should be able to avoid any fines.

Most fines are going to be listed in guidelines set forward by the state, and the most common areas they look into are your advertising, licensing, disclosures, and office space. Keep in mind that some states have brick-and-mortar requirements, and they do require you to display your licenses.

Let's look at the major categories addressed in any audit. Below are pointers for dealing with each one, and examples of what they will be looking for that could potentially be a fineable action.

Advertising

They will look to make sure:

- Your states are properly listed on your website, including contact information and logos.
- Your NMLS number is properly displayed on all correspondence with consumers.
- Your NMLS number is included on your business card.
- Any advertising that discloses interest rates contains the proper APR disclosure.
- That you are only marketing in approved states.
- All advertising contains bona fide offers, and no teasers.

Licensing

They will look to make sure:

- All loan officers are properly licensed.
- All proper background checks have been performed.
- The branch license is current and active.
- Your company license is current and active.
- You have fulfilled the correct net-worth requirements for license status per state.
- Bonds have the correct amounts, and are in effect.
- Errors and Omissions Insurance is in place, if required.

Disclosures

Probably the most important area they'll cover, with disclosures they will look for:

- State-specific disclosures that need to be a priority.
- All signed RESPA documents.
- Your Attorney and Insurance Agent preference form, plus the proof you disclosed options to them.
- Whether all documents have been counter signed by the closing loan officer.
- The closing documents that need to be in the file in e-loan.

Keep in mind that most auditors are going to be there to work *with* you, but some will be there on behalf of the state to collect fines. Part of the budgets for most states include the fines they take in from the brokerages under their watch.

In summary, for the enterprising banker who's ready to come over to the world of a mortgage broker, I believe that the decision to do so is the smartest decision you can make, assuming you are already generating your own business. Even if you are not all the way there yet in terms of self-generated business, we have covered a number of topics and areas that you can use as tools to help properly market yourself. At a minimum, you should feel strong enough about your brand to move to a correspondent lender or a local mortgage brokerage shop, even if you are not immediately ready to be on your own.

The best move one can make is to place the opportunity to earn more money squarely on one's own shoulders. You are the captain of your own ship, and you should be able to reap the rewards of your work.

If you have any questions, or would like to add comments about my work, please e-mail me at info@jasonc-myers.com. Make sure to visit our website (www.jasonc-myers.com), where you can sign up for our weekly sales tips to help you build more business, and where you can also order other books in our series. Thank you for reading, and I look forward to your comments.

Remember to stay positive, and to keep working to create a bright future for yourself.

About the Author

Jason C. Myers has been featured on the Inc. 5000, a list of the fastest-growing private companies in the nation, in both 2012 and 2013. He lives in Charleston, South Carolina with his wife, two children, and golden retriever. He has owned his own mortgage company since 2008 and has over 15 years of experiences in the mortgage industry. In 2013 his company did over $350 million in loan volume and $12 million in revenue.

67497555R00110

Made in the USA
Lexington, KY
13 September 2017